Making an Impact:

History Makers
Of the
Arkansas River Valley

Celebrate! Maya Project

Red Engine Press
Fort Smith, Arkansas

Cover Art by Tammy Nguyen
Cover Design by David King

Library of Congress Control Number: 2025936213

ISBN: 979-8-9985192-0-8

Introduction

A New Chapter in Southwest Arkansas Region History

The Celebrate! Maya Project is proud of the collective work of the Southwest Arkansas Region planning committee and Fort Smith School Districts, in coordinating this Writing History Project. We are especially proud that we can create partnerships with communities and school districts around the state to chronicle rich and often untold stories of men and women we call "History Makers."

Arkansas' history is rich and unique, including the rich history of the southwest region of Arkansas. Inside this part of the state has lived and continues to live, endless numbers of unsung heroes. We are proud to share some of these unsung heroes' stories in this book which honors their lives, their works, their struggles and their achievements.

Our collective history is what makes Arkansas the unique state that it is. Arkansas' Southwest region's history— from its birth, through its conflicts and its re-invention of itself – is what makes the region stand out from the rest of the state. Arkansas' young and old deserve to know their heritage and the people who helped pave the way for today. Many of these men and women will not be found in our history books. Some of their names will never be spoken outside their communities. Yet, their contributions, their lives and their stories are worthy of sharing here.

Making an Impact: History Makers of the Arkansas River Valley is just one chapter in Arkansas' southwest region's rich history. This chapter, however, includes stories that are invaluable to the community and the state. Stories that represent extraordinary men and women whose life work has impacted Arkansas' southwest region's growth and positive change.

> History cannot give us a program for the future, but it can give us a fuller understanding of ourselves, and of our own common humanity, so that we can face the future better. — Robert Penn Warren, American poet, author and literary critic

The student-scholars who participated in our writing history workshops, and the men and women who were interviewed, have, together, created an amazing document of which all of Arkansas should be proud.

This book captures the unique history of southwest Arkansas, focusing on the stories of unsung heroes who have contributed to the region's development. It emphasizes the importance of recognizing and sharing these narratives to help educate future generations about their heritage. This collective history is vital to understanding the identity of Arkansas. Moreso, it is a wonderful opportunity to honor the region's history through community engagement and storytelling efforts.

The men and women featured in this book – community and political leaders, public servants, artists, and more—represent the deep history of southwest Arkansas. It is our hope that both students and the general public will find this book helpful in understanding who we are as Arkansans.

Congratulations to the community planning committee who made this project a reality. Your work and this book beautifully honors Arkansas, and the distinctive history of its southwest region.

—Janis F. Kearney, Celebrate! Maya Project

Table of Contents

Mr. Jerry H. Moore, M.Ed.

Dr. Martin Luther King, Jr. once said, "Change will not come if we wait for some other person or some other time. We are the ones we've been waiting for."

Mr. Jerry H. Moore was born on April 26, 1949, in Kansas City, Kansas. He was raised by his mother's parents, Doyle and Eva Moore in Huntington, Arkansas.

Moore's life has included many firsts. He was one of the first of a group of students to integrate Mansfield Schools in 1962. "Going to Mansfield School was a great experience. We had no troubles between the White and Black students and the teachers were fair to us," Moore said. He was the first African American student elected to the Student Council, and the first African American member of the National Beta Club (NBC) at Mansfield High School, and the State of Arkansas before graduating in 1968. Moore said, "The National Beta Club had projects that the Honor Students would participate in; for instance, ballgames and community events. NBC oversaw the Honor Assembly every nine weeks. I graduated twelfth in ranking among forty-nine students."

By Mallory Jordan - eleventh-grade scholar at Northside High School

Moore graduated from Westark Community College in Fort Smith in 1970, and from the University of Arkansas at Fayetteville in 1991 with degrees in History and Sociology. He taught Sociology and Black History at Northside High School for eight years. Moore fondly stated, "My time at Northside was the start of my new life in shaping young minds and dealing with old teachers if I was good enough to be there." He taught Sociology and Arkansas History.

Later, Moore worked in the Student Support Service Trio Program for the U.S. Department of Education Grant Program for Low Income and First-Generation Students in College at the University of Arkansas - Fayetteville. He served as Upward Bound Director at Northwest Arkansas Community College from 2003–2014 and as an instructor in General Sociology from 2001–2024 in Bentonville, Arkansas.

In 1981, Moore appeared in the CBS Mini-Series, *The Blue and the Gray* filmed in Northwest Arkansas. He co-authored *No-Smoke, No Soot, No Clinker* in 1974. He has been published in *The Key* of the South Sebastian County Historical Society and formerly served as its president. Later in life, he'd be the first African American to host his radio talk show titled *Moore Talk* from 1997–2000 in Northwest Arkansas. Moore said, "A variety of topics covered all parts of a person's life that people could call in and share thoughts. In each program, a guest discussed their area of interest on the local, state, and national levels. The show was for everyone, not just for a particular group based on age, race, gender, social status, religious belief, education basis, or even political party."

Major Accomplishments

- Honorary Fellow for Life at the International College of Medical Technologies.

- Outstanding Young Man of America in 1976 and 1989 in recognition by the U.S. Junior Chamber Leadership Training, a service organization for people ages eighteen to forty.

- Founding member of Living Waters United Methodist Church in Centerton, Arkansas, and he has served as its first Lay Leader and Lay Minister for over ten years.

- Served as Arkansas Conference Chair of the committee working with the Native American Ministry in the United Methodist Church from 1995–2000 and from 2008–2012.

Ms. Sherry Lee (Brown) Toliver – Author, Journalist, History Maker

Former board member of the Fort Smith Museum of History, five-year commissioner of the Fort Smith City Park Department, member of the Democratic Women of Sebastian County, member of the Unity Missionary Baptist Church, former president of the Lincoln Alumni Association: these are all titles that Sherry Lee (Brown) Toliver holds. When questioned about her hobbies and pastimes, she exclaimed, "I don't have spare time!" Looking at her list of accomplishments, it is evident that she is busy.

Sherry Lee (Brown) Toliver was born on July 26th, 1944, in Kansas City, Missouri. Despite being born in the *Show-Me State*, she currently resides in Arkansas. The mother of two daughters, Toliver has lived in Texas, Kansas, and Missouri. Although Ms. Toliver has held a wide variety of positions, they all span back to one place—Fort Smith, Arkansas. She shares that her greatest accomplishment has been keeping the history of Lincoln High School—Fort Smith's historic African American high school. Ms. Toliver has made significant contributions to

By Tooba Sehr – twelfth-grade scholar at Southside High School

preserving the history of many students and people who walked through its halls through her penmanship and commitment to memorializing their stories.

Growing up, Ms. Toliver knew the now *Natural State* as the *Land of Opportunities*. When asked about this, she highlighted how ironic the nickname was. "When I was younger, my classmates would say that the first opportunity they were going to take was to get out of Arkansas," she laughed. Nonetheless, Fort Smith, Arkansas, was Ms. Toliver's home. She knew that no matter where life took her, she eventually would return.

Staying true to her word, she did return to Fort Smith. Highlighting the history of Fort Smith has been an important part of her life, including Lincoln High School, which was the former African American high school in Fort Smith, open from 1892 to 1966. Throughout its years, more than six thousand students walked the halls, and more than two hundred teachers taught there.[Horn] To preserve its history, Toliver and her best friend started the *Lincoln Echo* newspaper. They used a computer lab at a Fort Smith Community Center with no money, no education, and no typewriter. In the beginning, they were discouraged by onlookers. "Someone told me, "What are you going to put in it? Recipes?". They laughed at the idea that two women could run a newspaper. Despite this, the *Lincoln Echo* newspaper ran for eight years under Ms. Toliver, showcasing her dedication to the craft of education. Although Toliver faced many hurdles, she holds the accomplishment of authoring the longest-running newspaper in all of Arkansas.

Not only did Toliver start a newspaper, but she co-wrote a book about Lincoln High School with her friend and former classmate Barbara Meadows in 2015 to preserve the history of the school. The book is in every branch of the Fort Smith Public Library.

Their book is also featured in many other publications, including the *Fort Smith Historical Journal*. Toliver herself served on the board of the Fort Smith Museum of History for several years. She is dedicated to keeping the histories of the things before her and shares that her proudest achievements have been the book and newspaper. She excitedly says, "Because of the newspaper and book... they call me a historian. They gave me a title!"

While she is labeled as a history maker, she is also a history preserver. When asked about her title as a historian, she answered, "It's important to have a title so that people know that I'm a resource and a place to come for information." The most fulfilling part of her job is when she sees the actual effect of her work. She says, "People come to me to see if their family went to Lincoln High School or what class they were a part of." She also posts on Facebook about the history of Fort Smith. "There are so many contacts and so many interesting people," she exclaims. Highlighting the importance of connection, she emphasizes that "I wouldn't have met these people without this project."

Being booked doesn't prevent Sherry Toliver from connecting with people. She gets together once a month for lunch with her friends and classmates from high school. She also enjoys Pokeno. "It's like a big old bingo card and if you have a king of spades, you cover it. It's a good fellowship group," Toliver clarifies. She is also an active member at her local church, where she hosts a Bible study.

Through all of Sherry Lee (Brown) Toliver's experiences, we learn the importance of keeping history. When asked about her best advice for future history-makers, she advised, "Think before you speak and always be kind. I set out for no accomplishment, but I set out to inform so no one forgets." Ms. Toliver is a very influential person, and her grit will encourage the next generation of students, readers, and people alike to explore their past and the past of others, too.

Works Cited

Horn, Emily. "2024 Lincoln High School Reunion Spans Generations to Carry On a Rich Legacy." *Fort Smith Arkansas*, 9 August 2024, https://www.discoverfortsmith.com/articles/post/2024-lincoln-high-school-reunion /#:~:text=FORT%20SMITH%2C%20Ark.&text=Lincoln%20High%20School%20graduated%20its,integrated%20and%20was%20demolished%20thereafter. Accessed 4 March 2025.

Toliver, Sherry L. "Remembering Elm Grove Park." *Fort Smith Times Record*, 7 October 2018, https://www.swtimes.com/story/opinion/columns/guest/2018/10/07/remembering-elm-grove-park/9623654007/. Accessed 4 March 2025.

Floyd and Sue Robison – Historical Actors, Writers, Builders

From the courthouse to the schoolhouse and beyond, the ways that Floyd and Sue Robison have contributed to Fort Smith's history and community are far from fictional. The couple have been married for twenty-three years and have spent nearly that amount of time portraying Judge Issac Parker and his wife Mary in various events hosted by the Fort Smith Museum of History and other organizations. They are both natives of Fort Smith, born in 1950 and 1951, respectively. They are dedicated to preserving Fort Smith's history and educating people about what is and is not true. Through their time as judge and wife, they have learned a lot about how to present history in the true way that it happened and, in Sue's words, "How to politely tell people they're wrong." The Robisons are committed to bringing history to life and getting people engaged with the history of their community.

For both Robisons, interest in history started early. Sue recalls memories of her grandmother's house on North Sixth Street, which sparked her captivation with local history. "I remember walking the neighborhood and hearing stories about Belle Grove School, the Clayton family, the first house in town with electricity. All those things were around my grandmother's house. I was fascinated." An interest in history first began

By Lucas White - ninth-grade scholar at Southside High School

for Floyd when his father and uncles would tell him stories of World War II (WWII).

Their education and careers have taught them valuable lessons. Sue graduated from Northside High School in 1969. Floyd went to Southside High School as one of the first students to attend the school, graduating in 1968. After graduating high school, Sue attended the local Westark Community College (now the University of Arkansas - Fort Smith) and got a degree in journalism with an associate degree in communication.

Floyd joined the Navy after high school, serving with a helicopter unit known as the Seawolves. He was stationed in Binh Thuy, Vietnam, and celebrated his twenty-first birthday in the country. When describing his time there, he said, "Our function was considered air attack and support for PT boat forces and land forces. We also did retrievals, which means we went into hostile areas to bring out wounded or other individuals." When interviewed, Mr. Robison didn't have any specific stories that he wanted to share but said he would like it noted that the civilians he came into contact with were kind, generous people. He also mused, "Probably facing the daily challenges in Vietnam was the greatest upheaval in my life, but it also taught teamwork and unity in a way no other experience could."

After leaving the Navy, Floyd studied drafting in college, also at Westark. When he graduated, he began working for Arkansas Best Freight and remained with the company for thirty-five years. Sue took a job copywriting commercials for KFSM-TV in Fort Smith. She spent seventeen years with the company, eventually working her way up to producing live programming. She left that job to work with the *Times Record* newspaper for five years before it shut down, and after she found a position working for the local United Way agency. She learned a lot from these changes in her life, stating "Changes in career and family taught me to adjust and to trust in my own abilities." The couple were married in 2003, both having daughters from previous marriages. Sue's daughter, Ann, was born in 1974 and Floyd's daughter, Heather, was born in 1975.

The Robisons have expressed their shared love of Fort Smith's history and the city itself in many ways. Their first volunteer project together was in the late 1990s when they were both members of the Scots on the Border Club in Fort Smith. They were put in charge of building games for the children's area of the Scottish Games and Gathering, which was an event that the club hosted for five years. Floyd began volunteering at the Fort Smith National Historic Site in 2000, where he was part of the cannon crew. He also became part of a rifle regiment at the historic site and was eventually asked to present as Judge Parker for student groups. In 2002, both Floyd and Sue were invited to help with children's programs at the Fort Smith Museum of History. They have continued to work on various projects with the museum for more than twenty years. They still work with school groups that tour the museum, and Floyd helps build displays, such as courtroom sets and new desks in the media room. He also built the skiff, which is a replica of the first boat to land in Fort Smith.

Keelboat Landing

Even after both retired in 2014, the Robisons didn't stop loving history. The largest project that the two of them have worked on to date was the kick-off of the Fort Smith bicentennial celebration on Christmas Day 2016, where they oversaw landing a keelboat at the National Historic Site.

Together, they won the Fort Smith GRIT award for hospitality in 2014 and were second-place winners of the Arkansas Henry Award for tourism in 2018.

Sue has been given awards by the Arkansas Historical Association for three of her articles: "The Judge's Wife," a biography of Mary Parker, "A Century of Service," a review of Parker Elementary School in Fort Smith, and "The Task Performed by the Organization," a review of the German Prisoners of War held at Camp Chaffee during WWII. In 2024, the duo published a coloring book titled *The Little Judge* that was given out to children by the museum. The drawings were made by Floyd, and the book was written by Sue. They both continue to work on volunteer projects to this day, with several events and contributions lined up for the near future.

Throughout their lives, Floyd and Sue Robison have contributed to the preservation of Fort Smith's history by educating people in captivating, lively ways. Whether portraying historical figures, writing articles, or building props, the Robisons have made it their mission to educate and engage people in local history. They have brought Fort Smith's history to life in many ways, and they aren't done yet.

Sue & Floyd Robison - Actors

Major Accomplishment

- Cover design and artwork for the historical fiction book, *Julia and Maud* (2023).

Mrs. Denise Joan Johnson – Founder of The Housewives of Fort Smith

Surrounded by faith, family, and friends. Those are a few words used to describe Mrs. Denise Joan Johnson, who grew up as the youngest in a family of six siblings in Fort Smith, Arkansas. When Mrs. Johnson grew up in Fort Smith, she went to primarily black schools as many schools on the south side of town were not fully integrated. She ended up attending Howard Elementary School. At Howard, she went through grades one through six with her mother working at the school as a certified cook and manager for twenty-four years. Her love of school stems from being able to go to school and knowing her mother was right there beside her until she advanced to middle school.

After Howard, she went to Darby Middle School where integrated schools were just beginning. Her love of learning kept growing. She went to Northside High School as a member of the class of 1974. She earned her General Educational Development (GED) certification in 1975 at Peabody School. Mrs. Johnson says that her education is all because of her parents' love and unwavering support. She recalls, "They said we were poor, but I never really saw that because

By Tori Smith - eleventh-grade scholar at Southside High School

they provided everything we ever needed. From food to clothes, shelter, transportation, education, we had it all." While out of school, she met her husband, Herbert Johnson, with whom she married in 1991 and raised three children (Dedra, Shiron, and Maya'Neisha). In 2007, at the age of fifty-one, Mrs. Johnson decided to further her education, but then, unfortunately, Denise's mother's terminal illness made her trip to the University of Arkansas - Fort Smith a short one. However, she still has a passion for learning and said she is constantly reading and trying to learn everything the world has to offer.

The Housewives of Fort Smith

Mrs. Johnson submitted opinion articles to the local Fort Smith newspaper, *The Southwest Times Record*, under the column "How You See It." Mrs. Johnson is the Founder and President of The Housewives of Fort Smith, a Christian charitable group whose members routinely serve their community through their various endeavors. Her daughter Maya'Neisha is one of the biggest influences on her career because she is loving and gives great advice.

Additionally, she says being an ordained Seventh-Day Adventist Elder and working closely with her faith inspired her professional life. In Mrs. Johnson's life, having a career has increased her value and how she views the world because of the opportunities that came with her various career choices. Now, she is retired and working part-time at Harvest Time Tabernacle in the infant care room. She also spends her free time volunteering at Baptist Health as a chaplain.

One lesson she has learned in life is how to use her religious practices to cope with living in an unjust world. Mrs. Johnson said, "I had to learn through a lot of prayers and more faith and trust in God even though I was totally discouraged and in disbelief that God didn't answer my financial prayer the way I thought he should and would. What really gets me through this disappointment is still being and staying in his will. Also, I'm standing on his promise from July 18, 2024. 'I'm about to fully retire you and you will be set for the rest of your life.'"

As Denise Johnson reflected on life lessons, her advice to others is to do what you say you're going to do and to be the best at it. Furthermore, she believes that people should be the change they wish to see in others and always speak the truth. In Mrs. Johnson's free time, she writes, plays dominoes, bowls, walks, watches *Perry Mason*, and visits her elderly friends in their homes or nursing homes.

One of Mrs. Johnson's greatest accomplishments happened just a few years ago: "The year 2021 changed my life." Denise Johnson became closer than ever to her African roots after connecting with an engaged couple, the bride from Kenya and the groom from California. She was flown out to Seattle, Washington by the couple to officiate their wedding and got so close to the family that she considers the bride to be her adoptive daughter. She also has a godson/grandson that she went to visit recently. She was so touched and moved by the honor of marrying the two that she almost gave up a life in Fort Smith for a life in Seattle. However, she realizes that her family and life are in Arkansas, and she doesn't regret staying.

Denise & Daughters

Mr. Tracy B. Christian – Father, Husband, Steelworker, Volunteer

Tracy B. Christian, inspired by his faith, family, and goodwill, dedicates his life to helping people. Mr. Christian was born in Fort Smith, Arkansas, in 1962. He graduated from Northside High School in 1980 and went straight into the workforce. Mr. Christian attended Westark Community College, now known as the University of Arkansas - Fort Smith (UAFS).

Family means a lot to Mr. Christian. He and his wife Nichelle have four daughters, and five grandchildren. They also had a son, Aaron, who had special needs due to health complications when he was six weeks old and sadly died in 2002 at the age of thirteen. Aaron made a huge impact on others.

Mr. Christian said that even though his son couldn't partake in some activities, he could still laugh and bring their family joy and innocence. For him, his son is his biggest hero. Mr. Christian also took inspiration and influence from his

By Elizabeth Fore - tenth-grade scholar at Southside High School

grandfathers, Mr. Kill Kinnard and Mr. C.J. Christian Sr., his wife, and his uncle Calvin Christian, who helped him get his job at Gerdau Macsteel.

Tracy Christian has worked at Gerdau Macsteel for over forty years. Gerdau is a global company that trades steel and other raw materials. Mr. Christian was one of a collective group of employees at his job that organized to become a bargaining unit. Once chartered, they were named United Steelworkers (USW) Local #9542 Union. "Bargaining units fight for fair wages, safe working conditions, and serve as a voice on the job for the membership," said Christian. The USW Local #9452 received a Certificate of Charter Affiliation with the USW on February 29, 2000, and Mr. Christian served as a president for over twenty years.

When I asked Mr. Christian what he thought his greatest accomplishment was, he replied, "Helping people." So when he is not working, he's volunteering. Mr. Christian serves on the Lincoln Youth Service Center board. The late Mr. Alvin Bradley Sr., the late Lawrence E. Tidwell Sr., and the late Mr. Paul Christian founded the Lincoln Youth Service Center. He also volunteers at The Arc for the River Valley. which serves adults with intellectual disabilities. They provide "advocacy, education, and recreation" such as weekly classes and activities for members, including movies, outdoor activities, bowling, art, science classes, and cooking classes.

Alvin Bredley, Sr. &
Lawrence Tidwell, Sr.

STEPS Family Resource Center is another organization where Mr. Christian volunteers. STEPS currently offers nurturing parenting, anger management, co-parenting, and life skills classes for individuals and families in the River Valley and surrounding areas. Through his volunteerism, Mr. Christian strives to make a positive impact by serving and supporting others.

Mr. Christian's advice is don't compromise your integrity, don't lie, and be true to yourself. "These are essential ideas to always keep in mind as you live your life and become your own person," he said. I asked him if he had any advice for others and he said to not focus on making money; know what God wants you to do and do what you love. Knowing these things can help you become a better person and help others. Volunteering and helping his community are very important to Mr. Christian. By listening to his heart and doing what he loves, Mr. Tracy Christian has become a kind, goodhearted, caring person that everyone should aspire to emulate.

Mr. Tom Shay – Author, Entrepreneur, Community Leader

Tom Shay's life exemplifies the power of perseverance, passion, and the pursuit of meaningful connections.

Born in Fort Smith, Arkansas, in 1952, Shay's path was shaped by the strong influence of his parents, who showed him the values of hard work and dedication. Today, Shay is a professional speaker and author of twelve books, inspiring others through his experiences and insights. His journey is marked by risk, resilience, and the courage to embrace uncertainty. His experiences demonstrate the importance of following one's passion despite the challenges.

Shay's educational journey began at Ballman Elementary School in Fort Smith. He continued at Dardanelle High School and Hendrix College in Conway, Arkansas. Shay is a life-long learner. He now is attending classes at the University of Arkansas - Fort Smith (UAFS). Mr. Shay

By Kassidy Badger - tenth-grade scholar at Northside High School and Mr. Tom Shay

acknowledges, "My attendance at UAFS is something I am doing now as I enjoy the learning challenge."

Throughout his career, Shay has credited his parents as the most significant influencers in his life. Their encouragement and belief in Shay gave him the confidence to pursue new opportunities and face challenges head-on. While Shay's parents gave him a strong foundation, it was a salesman, Mr. Dennis Chappell, who ultimately convinced him to step into the world of public speaking: a decision that changed the course of his life. This turning point allowed Shay to develop a career that brought him meaningful experiences, valuable connections, and the courage to take risks.

Shay's career as a professional speaker has provided him with remarkable opportunities to meet new people and share his insights with audiences across various industries. His work required bravery, as there was no guarantee of success when he first began. Despite the uncertainty, Shay's passion for his craft kept him motivated. He often reflects on his journey by summarizing Mark Twain's philosophy: A man who has had a cat by the tail knows a lot more than the man who read about it. For Shay, this equates to his belief that real-life experiences are the greatest teachers: a lesson he often shares with his audiences.

Mr. Shay has an extreme passion for volunteerism and giving back. His greatest achievements are creating the Sand Lizard Foundation and

The Sand Lizard Foundation Board of Directors

the True Grit Trail. He is one of the founders and the current president of the Sand Lizard Foundation. Over the past six years Sand Lizard Foundation has awarded over forty-three thousand dollars to Dardanelle graduates. The Sand Lizard Foundation was honored with the 2025 Member of the Year award by the Dardanelle Area Chamber of Commerce.

"The True Grit Trail is an organization that promotes businesses in western Arkansas and southwestern Oklahoma, which is the setting for Charles Portis' book, *True Grit*," said Shay. The fictional character, Mattie Ross, tells the stories of villains and heroes of the 1880s.

When asked about his greatest accomplishments, Shay humbly stated that he's still achieving them and remains proud of the successes

Unveiling of the True Grit mural in Dardanelle, Arkansas

he has already experienced. Rather than focusing on past achievements, he continues to ask himself, "What more can I do?" This mindset drives him to keep learning, growing, and contributing to the world around him. His dedication to continual improvement echoes his belief that success is not a destination but an ongoing journey.

The main lessons Shay has learned in life are to "be well-grounded" and "stick to your principles." He strongly believes that success comes from maintaining integrity and staying true to one's values, no matter the obstacles. In his words, "The world isn't going to hand you anything; you must work for your achievements." This belief has shaped his approach to both life and his career. By holding fast to these principles, Shay has not only improved his own life but also paved the way for others to succeed. His dedication to empowering others through his writing, speaking, and mentorship demonstrates his commitment to creating opportunities for those willing to work hard and stay true to themselves.

In conclusion, Tom Shay's life is defined by courage, passion, and perseverance. Influenced by his parents and guided by a pivotal mentor, Mr. Jack Rice, Shay built a career that not only brought him personal fulfillment but also inspired others to pursue their goals fearlessly. His story serves as a reminder that success requires effort, integrity, and a commitment to lifelong growth. Through his books, speeches, and unwavering drive to improve the world around him, Tom Shay continues to leave a lasting impact on those who follow his example.

Major Achievements

- Business Management Expert, Profits Plus Solutions for Small Business
- Sand Lizard Foundation
- Creator of the True Grit Trail

Works Cited

Raya, Daisy. "Kassidy Badger and Mr. Tom Shay Interview Image." 25 Jan. 2025. Accessed 25 Jan. 2025.

Shay, Tom. "Unveiling of the True Grit Mural." True Grit Trail, 7 Jun. 2023, www.truegrittrail.com/. Accessed 18 Mar. 2025.

Shay, Tom. "Members of Sand Lizard Foundation Board." True Grit Trail, 28 Jan. 2025, www.sandlizardfoundation.com/. Accessed 18 Mar. 2025.

Dr. Steve-Felix Belinga – General Neurologist, Father, and Philanthropist

Impossible is just a sum of possibilities ~Dr. Steve-Felix Belinga.

Born in Cameroon, Central Africa, Dr Belinga grew up very connected to his family, influencing him in such a way that he carries the life lessons in this motto. Devoted Christians, his father and maternal grandfather influenced him to always give to others, even when there wasn't much to offer, stating, "Give and God gives back." This would segue into his adult life when he began his philanthropic journey with The Belinga Foundation, ultimately making history in Fort Smith

Dr. Belinga's life was heavily influenced by his family. For example, his aunt taught him English and shared music, like from Louis Armstrong, to help him learn English in an entertaining way. That exposure planted the seed of curiosity. Smiling, he says, "I have to say water (water is pronounced with the T emphasized) I have to say that 'T' because she made sure I said that T when I was somewhere between nine and ten." Dr Belinga's fascination with the brain started young and grew into a

By Josianne Gentry - twelfth-grade scholar at Southside High School

passion. His father, knowing about his son's talent, and the quality of education in America, decided that his eldest son would move to America to be a doctor, essentially telling him, "You are going to be a physician in America or get out of my house." He reflects that his father was the most influential person in his life because he pushed his perceived limits further so that he could reach his full potential. Additionally, his grandfather influenced his pursuit of God's work. He taught him to, "do something right every single day and you will never have to regret that you lived, even in old age.

Dr. Belinga moved to America in March 1998 at the age of eighteen and finished his undergraduate college in two and a half years at Georgia State University (in Atlanta), a truly difficult task. However, Dr. Belinga says it was easy compared to Medical School. "In college, I would challenge myself; however, Medical School challenged me way more than I could challenge myself." Attending Medical School at Washington University in Saint Louis School of Medicine (the Harvard of the Midwest), Dr. Belinga struggled to find support in a program so demanding. In the most difficult moment, his father's influence manifested as a small saying, "The only limit you have is the limit you put on yourself." These words carried him through.

Belinga served his residency at the University of Kentucky Chandler Medical Center in Lexington, where he had to be a student and a doctor, with virtually no time to study. Nights were taken up by calls where he had to skip sleep for reasons other than just studying /learning. Residency, he said, was the most formative experience of his career and shaped his life even today in good and bad ways. Lack of sleep became chronic insomnia. While many people would say this trait is bad, Belinga says he is stronger because of it. Even when he is tired, he can perform highly intellectual activities in stressful situations like staying vigilant and making conscious decisions, often lifesaving, regardless of the time at night. That is the hallmark of a good doctor. "Wake me up at any time of the night; I will give you the right answer."

University of Kentucky
Medical Center

Outside of work, Dr. Belinga has three children; a thirteen-year-old son named Elric, a twelve-year-old daughter named Mercedes, and an eleven-year-old daughter named Jocelyne. Being a father is his greatest accomplishment, "They're my greatest joy and my greatest light, even in the darkest moments and the deepest fears." His children's happiness reminds him that no matter what achievements he earns; "will it ever make [him] as happy as [his] children are?" He explains that it gives him pride that his children are happy and that he can influence the next generation through them. He credits most of his accomplishments, including his children, to God, allowing him to be a humble servant in His plan.

Dr. Belinga owns three clinics under the his foundation located in Russellville, Arkansas; Fort Smith, Arkansas; and Wagoner, Oklahoma. A fourth clinic is in the works for Dallas, Texas. His clinics embody his 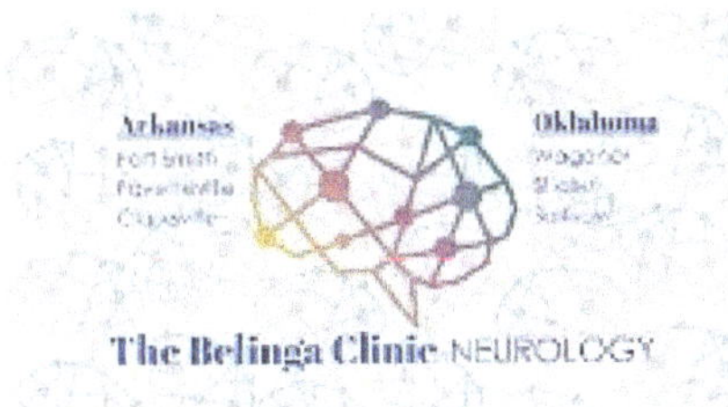

motto *Impossible is just a sum of possibilities*. He constantly is looking to improve and strengthen his impact in the world, "What else can I turn from impossible to possible? That's why I get up every single day; how many more patients can I see? What structure can my clinic have? What impact can my foundation have, and what more can my staff do even when they don't believe they can do it?"

The Belinga Foundation's goal is to unlock the potential in others by "lighting that spark or planting that seed." The foundation is not for teaching, he explains, it's about guiding them broadly. It points those with often hidden talents in the right direction, so they can believe in themselves, and thus improve until they are great.

Dr. Belinga's job gives him the financial ability to give generously to people in need through his clinics and charity. He and his family travel to Africa often to help teach important lessons and give to the underprivileged. When he is not busy with patients, he gives money to many non-profits, including many in Fort Smith. Dr. Belinga and his clinic are involved in many activities that strengthen Fort Smith such as the Fort Smith Round Table, Fort Smith Boxing Club, Fort Smith Boys and Girls Club, Fort Smith Civics Society, and many others. Dr. Belinga is not only a history maker in Fort Smith—but also in the world.

Dr. Belinga's life teaches lessons he uses to inspire and help others through struggles. One is that "Humans are meant to suffer, and if you accept that, if you believe that, then everything else is bliss." This comes from the idea, he explains, that if you prepare yourself for obstacles, then they feel less big when you encounter them so that, "it's actually pretty easy the rest of the time." With that same preparedness, you can give it your all and overcome most obstacles. "True bliss is beyond all obstacles," he argues. If you can separate your self-worth from the idea of failure, you learn from it because "Success is not as good a teacher as failure."

Overall, Dr. Steve-Felix Belinga helps many people in Fort Smith, creating history through his work in neurology and philanthropy. He explains that "understanding the brain is critical when you want to unleash somebody's potential." The brain is very smart even when someone doesn't see what the brain sees. He guides people through unlocking their potential by what he explains as having a conversation with their brains. Starting with children in Fort Smith, his foundation hopes to expand to help adults. This understanding of the brain makes him a crucial neurologist in Fort Smith, helping to bring out the best in each individual he encounters.

Mrs. Katherine Brown – Heroine and Community Activist
(March 14, 1915 – June 7, 2010)

Mrs. Katherine Jones Brown and her sister,
Mrs. Ruby Jones Young Thomas
(Photograph courtesy of Nichelle Christian)

Do you act, pause, or do nothing when you see an issue that needs to be addressed, and how does it make you feel?

Maya Angelou once said, "When you do nothing you feel overwhelmed and powerless. But when you get involved, you feel the sense of hope and accomplishment that comes from knowing that you are working to make things better."

Katherine Brown was named Alpha Omega Jones at birth on March 14, 1915, by her parents Albert and Georgia "Teed" Jones in Huntington, Arkansas during the Great Depression. Her dad was a coal miner, and her mother was a homemaker. Brown was the sibling of 4 sisters and 2 brothers. She attended Phillis Wheatley Elementary School in Huntington during her youth. It was a two-room schoolhouse that served first through eighth-grade students. Brown was valedictorian of her class at Phillis Wheatley Elementary. In 1935, she completed her junior year at Lincoln High School in Fort Smith, Arkansas.

By Aiden Pope - tenth-grade scholar at Northside High School

"My grandmother told me that she did not like her birth name, so she changed it to Katherine," revealed Nichelle Christian, Brown's granddaughter. "That takes a strong sense of self-awareness to declare who you are as she did—I thought

As a young adult, Brown married Leroy W. Brown, Sr., and moved to Fort Smith where she completed her junior year at the historic Lincoln High School. Although she would have loved to continue her education, her life as a wife and mother took preeminence. They had two sons: Leroy W. Brown, Jr. and James E. Brown.

"Despite the impact of growing up during the Great Depression and having a clear understanding of her status in society as a colored woman, the realities of life did not dampen her spirit nor did it define her sense of self-worth and identity," according to her granddaughter, Nichelle Christian. "The most prominent life lesson, among many other lessons that my grandmother taught me was to be strong and to never compromise my moral beliefs to please others."

Katherine Brown used her wisdom, strength, and resilience to serve her family and community. When she saw a need, she used her ingenuity and connections with like-minded people within the community to meet that need. For instance, while she was serving as president of the Lincoln High School Parent-Teacher Association (PTA), the football team and the band needed uniforms. "My grandmother told me that the school system, which was segregated, offered their used band and football uniforms to Lincoln High School. I remember the look of distaste upon her face as she reflected on that experience," said Christian. "'We didn't want

Katherine Brown

their old uniforms. Our children deserved new uniforms, so the parents banded together and hosted fundraisers. Eventually, we purchased new uniforms for the football team and the band,'" Brown told her granddaughter.

James E. Brown

"My dad, James, played the saxophone in the Lincoln High School Band, and my uncle Leroy Jr. played on the football team. So meeting this need was not only for my grand-mother's children but for all the young people at Lincoln High School. My grandmother was adamant about her convictions regarding this matter." Brown told her granddaughter, "'We were not going to accept any hand-me-down uniforms.'"

Brown Family

In the words of the late Charlotte Tidwell, "'Katherine Brown became a professional entrepreneur for obtaining contributions in the colored community. Something that was unheard of in the small community of Fort Smith.'"

"It was 2003 when I sat in my grand-mother's den, looking through a box of old photographs, when I came across a black and white photograph of a beautiful group of women wearing long evening gowns, each holding a long, silky scarf. This is when I first learned about the Rainbow Girls, and their contributions to our African American community," said Christian. Katherine Brown was president of the Rainbow Girls Women's Auxiliary Club during the mid-1940s. The Rainbow Girls was a philanthropic, colored women's auxiliary club, and they raised funds to support the Twin City Colored Hospital that was located at 1717 Midland Boulevard in Fort Smith. "'We raised funds to purchase linens, toiletries, and other needed practical supplies for the hospital's patients,'"

The Rainbow Girls in 1943 (left to right): Easter Walker; Willie Hoffman; Verna Johnson; Paralee Wilson; Berta Jean Cook McCloud; Louella Edwards; Emma Murphy, mentor; Ruby Jones Young Thomas; Katherine Jones Brown, president; Elletrice McGill; and Beatrice Caldwell Malone. Mrs. Isabelle Bass was not present for the photograph.

(Photo courtesy of Nichelle Christian)

Christian remembered her grandmother sharing. The club dues were fifteen cents per meeting, and the Rainbow Girls met every two weeks.

"One might be shocked to hear that African Americans, in Fort Smith, once received medical care in the most unlikely places. The late Mrs. Euba Winton told me that a black man, who needed dental work, had a tooth pulled in the basement of the historic Mallalieu United Methodist Church. This was my childhood church," Christian revealed. "This is a major and unique part of our city's history that should not be forgotten." Before having a hospital to serve the medical needs of African Americans, it was not uncommon for dining room tables to sometimes be used as operating tables. After no longer being accommodated by Sparks Hospital's annex for colored people and being told to get a place of their own in 1931, W.A. Rowell, mortician, offered his Mortuary Parlors for surgeries. Seeing the medical need for the colored population, Dr. H.D. Thompson and Dr. Wright Hawkins obtained an abandoned building on North Fifth Street and founded the Border City Colored Hospital. Its first black nurse was Miss Ella Jones of Tennessee. Before the establishment of the Twin City Colored Hospital, Dr. Thompson would treat and perform surgeries on African American patients in his clinic and then send them home immediately to recuperate. Mr. W.A. Rowell donated two lots on North Eleventh Street. Some support came from the Men's Progressive Club. The City contracted the Works Progress Administration (WPA) to place a building on the property, and Twin City Hospital opened on January 1, 1941. The hospital struggled for necessities, and the Rainbow Girls answered the call to help fulfill that need.

"Charlotte F. Tidwell shared newspaper clippings that documented some of the history and the inequities within the healthcare system inside of our community, and included a portion of my grandmother's life story and her contributions in a book by Mrs. Tidwell wrote titled *The Legacy Continues: Katherine Jones Brown*. She gave the book to me and my family as a gift. History like this has the potential to be lost if it was not for people like Mrs. Tidwell, Mrs. Euba Winton, and many others who have passed the truths of our histories from one generation to the next," said Christian.

One of the most significant accomplishments of the Rainbow Girls was when they raised enough funds to purchase a blue neon sign to place atop the Twin City Colored Hospital. "According to my grandmother, they only had paid half the cost of the sign when it was placed at the hospital, and they soon raised the remaining funds to finalize the purchase," said Christian. "It was very dark on Midland

Boulevard at night, and this sign made it easier for patients, especially from surrounding cities, to locate the hospital at night."

"I do not believe I would have known about the Rainbow Girls or the significant impact they had on our community if I had not found and inquired about the beautiful photograph in my grandmother's cardboard box," Christian stated. "My grandmother did not talk much about the past. I am proud of my grandmother, and this entire group of women for their efforts supporting the needs of the African American community through their philanthropic work on behalf of the Twin City Colored Hospital in Fort Smith, Arkansas. In 2010, I was honored to share the story about the Rainbow Girls with my colleagues while I served as a member of the American Democracy Project while working at the University of Arkansas - Fort Smith (UAFS). My grandmother and Mrs. Isabell Bass were the last two living members of the Rainbow Girls when they were presented with Civic Engagement awards at UAFS for contributing to civil rights advocacy on January 19, 2010."

Dr. Billy Higgins, retired, Professor Emeritus of History at UAFS said, "My extensive interview with Ms. Katherine Brown occurred on January 13, 2010, in her home. I remember how gracious she and Ms. Bass were. Impressive to me were the extensive knowledge, the strength, and the good spirit of each of the women. They obviously thought so well of each other. Their lives because of their giving and forgiving nature seemed to be of great joy. They knew satisfaction in their continued service. Although discrimination was common in their era, they both knew how to get around it by looking for ways to help their community and deal effectively with the other separate society. At a UAFS gathering in the Reynolds Room, Dr. Paul B. Beran honored them for their historical role in Fort Smith not long after the interviews. There is a picture of that event in the *Journal of the Fort Smith Historical Society*."

Christian reflected on the recognition ceremony. "My grandmother and Mrs. Bass were thrilled and humbled for the honor placed upon them that day. I clearly remember my grandmother smiling and looking into my eyes saying, "'Nichelle, we have never been recognized for what we did.'"

"I can still visualize her smile, and the joy in her eyes that day. She was my hero!" Christian stated fondly.

The Rainbow Girls, a group of heroines, have left a legacy that their community, families, and friends can be proud of for generations to come!

Major Achievements

Phillis Wheatley Elementary School, Huntington, AR -
Valedictorian of her class (Grades 1 – 8)

Quinn Chapel AME Church
- Sponsored a fundraiser to liquidate the debt on the mortgage, and the pipe organ.

Past President of the Lincoln High School PTA - Played an instrumental role with her peers to support academic and extra-curricular activities.
- New uniforms for the Marching Band.
- New uniforms for the Football team.
- Commercial classes for Lincoln High School.

President of the Rainbow Girls
- Community Activist
- Civic Fund Raiser
- The Rainbow Girls Colored Women's Auxiliary Club was founded in the 1940s.
- Raised funds to support the operations and patients at the Twin City Colored Hospital.
- Honored as a recipient of the Civic Engagement Award by the American Democracy Project at the University of Arkansas - Fort Smith on January 19, 2020.

Mr. Billy D. Higgins – Retired, Professor Emeritus, History Department University of Arkansas - Fort Smith

Have you ever heard the saying "It's a small world"? It is a small world! Mr. Billy D. Higgins interviewed my great-great-grandmother, Katherine Brown, at her home on January 13, 2010, days before she and Mrs. Isabelle Bass were honored by the American Democracy Project at the University of Arkansas - Fort Smith (UAFS) for contributions they made on behalf of the Rainbow Girls, a Colored Women's Auxiliary Club to the Twin City Colored Hospital in Fort Smith, Arkansas during the 1940s. I was thirteen months old at the time. Who would have ever thought that I would one day interview Dr. Higgins?

Probably no one!

Mr. Billy D. Higgins was born on October 10, 1938, in Morrilton, Arkansas. He is married to Peggy, and they are the parents of Tim and Lea. "I had good experiences in education, Fort Smith Public Schools, and then Arkansas University and Vanderbilt University." reflected Higgins, who graduated with a Bachelor of Science (B.S.) degree from Boston College in

By Kylie Davis - tenth-grade scholar at Southside High School

1969 and earned a Doctor of Philosophy (Ph.D.) from Florida State University in 1973.

"I like life stories. I read biographies of presidents, and movie stars and stuff like that, so I like to know what they went through a long time ago. And then, I like to know what people are going through now. I don't know why. That's what interests me. People's stories. Whoever invented the printing press, whoever invented the banjo, whoever first cultivated okra, those were the people that influenced me," stated Mr. Billy D. Higgins. "Friends influenced me, teachers influenced me. I met your great-grandmother, Katherine Brown, and people like that greatly influenced how I saw the world and the people in it."

In earlier days, Mr. Higgins lived on a farm with his wife and two children. They attended a rural school before moving back to Fort Smith. Mr. Higgins served in the United States Air Force (USAF), "I was commissioned and was a navigator in cargo planes," he said, "During those years, I had a lot of different kinds of experiences, and all were valuable to me, and I met a lot of different kinds of people, all of whom were very valuable to me as well." Mr. Higgins clocked three thousand hours airtime while serving in the military. According to his website, billydhiggins.com, he once was a trans-oceanic navigator who was trained to use celestial fixes to plot the course of the piston-engine, low-speed, low-altitude airplane that has been referred to as the backbone of the Military Air Transportation Service (MATS) from 1949 through 1974."

Cover of Billy's Book

Mr. Higgins has accomplished a great deal in his life. For example, he is an author, and his published works include, *The Barling Darling: Hal Smith in American Baseball*, *Navigating the C-124 Globemaster: In the Cockpit of America's First Strategic Heavy-Lift Aircraft*, and many more! Additionally, one of the most significant things he did was teach students geography and history for twenty-eight years at UAFS. He recalls, "We kind of bonded the people you taught with and even with some students who went on and you'd hear from 'em later and share some things." He is a member of the Fort Smith Boys & Girls Club Scholarship Committee. The scholarship is given to students who volunteer at the club. "It's not a full scholarship, but it's two or three thousand dollars each semester." Mr. Higgins explained that UAFS matches whatever the club awards to students. He takes pride in the fact that "you kind of double it by staying at home here."

Mr. Higgins's advice to young people is to "Try to be of service to the people around you, even if it is just in the neighborhood… just don't be driven by money." Now retired, Mr. Higgins is relishing in the things he enjoys, like listening to music, playing pickleball or golf, and continuing to pore into the lives of young people through volunteerism. "There's nothing better than watching a good team, and they all rely on each other, and they know how to pass and do assists and all of that," he said. Mr. Higgins is passing the mantle of his in-depth knowledge of history, inspiring others to learn and preserve the stories about individuals for present and future generations!

Works Cited

Higgins, Dr. Billy D. *Navigating the C-124 Globemaster: In the Cockpit of America's First Strategic Heavy-Lift Aircraft*. Billy D. Higgins Welcome to Billydhiggins.Com, 26 Jul. 2019, billydhiggins.com. Accessed 18 Mar. 2025.

Dr. A. Naseer Adjei, MD, FACC, FSCAI – Chief of Cardiology, Baptist Hospital

"A 2021 report by the Association of American Medical Colleges found that only four-point-two percent of cardiologists are African American. An earlier study, published in 2019 in The Journal of the American Medical Association (JAMA) had similar findings, revealing that African American doctors made up only three percent of the cardiologist workforce." NBC News reported.

Dr. Adjei is the Chief of Cardiology at Baptist Hospital in Fort Smith, Arkansas. "I chose the field of Cardiology because it was an interesting and intriguing thing to me when I was in training. I felt I would enjoy it and indeed I love what I do! The subject of heart disease is complex and has a more sentimental meaning to a lot of people. There is so much that can be done to treat heart disease, but unfortunately, heart disease is the leading cause of death in the world," Dr. Adjei revealed.

By Aiden Pope - tenth-grade scholar at Northside High School

Dr. Adjei was born in November of 1966, and began his journey in Ghana, Africa. He was raised there until he finished high school. Dr. Adjei explained that education in Ghana is "The British Way of learning." He explained, "Medical school is six years, unlike the traditional four years in the U.S. They go straight from high school to medical school training."

He attended medical school in Ankara Turkey and later completed an internship and residency at Columbia University College of Physicians and Surgeons, Harlem Hospital Center, New York, New York. Adjei specializes in angioplasty /stent placement, left and right heart catheterization, coronary and peripheral artery angiography, intra-aortic balloon pump insertion, and Impella placement. "One of the most important surgeries that I perform is coronary—when somebody has a heart attack and one of the arteries is clogged up, and I go to unclog the artery and put a stent in there immediately that usually saves their life and also relieves their pain and suffering right away and that gives me the best job satisfaction," Adjei said. "In Arkansas, heart disease remains the number one cause of death and we made progress, but we are still lagging behind the rest of the country, so we still need a lot of education in terms of symptom recognition, early arrival to the emergency room, and activation of emergency services so that care can begin treatment as soon as possible, and this can lead to saving lives and decreasing the risk of death and long-term consequences of heart attacks in communities."

The Adjei Family

The most influential person in his life was his uncle. His uncle was a Professor of Political Science and History. Adjei said his uncle was very interested in his education and well-being.

In his free time, Dr. Adjei does several activities for recreation. He said, "My leisure time is spent gardening. Also, I love water sports, so I spend a lot of time at the lake with my family during the summer. Traveling around the world providing healthcare is something that I'm passionate about." Ultimately, his family members' lives revolve around the healthcare system. Adjei said, "My younger sister is a registered nurse in New York City. And of course, my wife is also a registered nurse, so we have a few of us in the healthcare industry.

When asked about the most important thing people should do to maintain a good heart, Dr. Adjei said, "One of the most important things that people need to do to maintain good health is to be consciously aware of it. We are surrounded by many things that are not good for us in terms of high-energy/high-calorie foods that we eat. Lack of exercise and just not paying attention to our overall health. One of the things you need to do is exercise. It doesn't mean just going to the gym. It means walking or taking time to be conscious that you're doing something for your body, including healthy and mindful eating. Having a routine medical check-up and maintaining good blood pressure. Of course, you know about checking blood pressure, checking for diabetes, and maintaining a healthy cholesterol level are some of the things that can be done, including a healthy body weight."

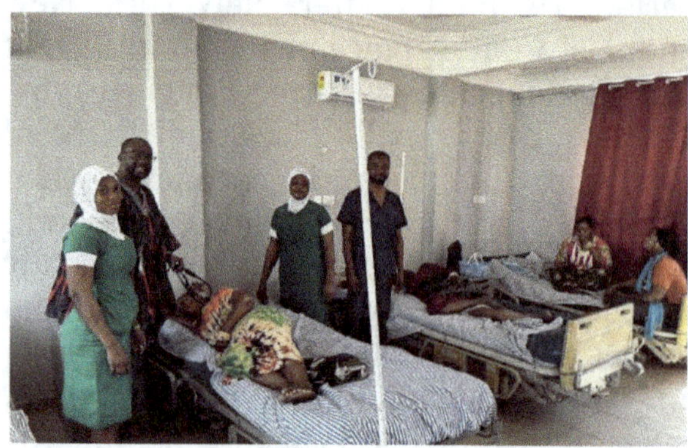

Dr. Adjei and a team of nurses in the city of Tamale, Northern Ghana

Major Achievements

- Completed his Interventional Cardiology Fellowship in 2003 at the State University of New York, Downstate Medical Center, and Staten Island University Hospital, New York.

- Specializes in Coronary Angioplasty/Stent placement.

- Annual Heart Health Exposition at Baptist Hospital.

- Travelling globally to treat patients.

Dr. Carolyn Mosley, PhD, RN, CS, FAAN, ANEF

We discover what we are made of when life's circumstances seem unfair. Some people give up on their hopes and dreams while others push through to achieve them. Dr. Carolyn Mosley has never been one to give up!

Dr. Carolyn Mosley's life is a powerful testament to inner strength and determination. She faced countless obstacles throughout her life but refused to let them define her or her future. She worked hard to build a successful career in nursing, and she later became the Dean of the College of Health Sciences at the University of Arkansas - Fort Smith. Mosley's dedication to the field of Healthcare Education helped open doors for future generations of medical professionals, especially those from underrepresented backgrounds. Now retired, Dr. Mosley's story proves that determination and education can create change and inspire others to push forward, no matter the challenges.

By Kassidy Badger - tenth-grade scholar at Northside High School

Dr. Carolyn Mosley was born on November 2, 1952, in New Orleans, Louisiana. She grew up during the era of segregation, facing numerous challenges that could have taken her off the path that she was destined for. While studying Nursing at Louisiana State University, she endured racism and other harsh treatment at the hands of some of her professors. On one occasion, other students defended Mosley by challenging a professor's cruel treatment of her. Despite these challenges, Dr. Mosley refused to give up while facing adversity.

She endured one of her greatest challenges when a very destructive, tropical storm called Hurricane Katrina slammed New Orleans and left her homeless. Still, she pushed forward and got through this very tough time. "It was a devastating thing to go through at the time," Mosley recalls.

Despite the heartache, her career brought her immense value, allowing her to achieve leadership roles such as serving on the Baptist Health Corporate Board, Court Appointed Special Advocates, Girls Incorporated of Fort Smith, president of Chi Eta Phi Sorority, and Epsilon Nu Chapter of Sigma Theta Tau International Honor Society for Nurses. Mosley credits those who doubted her as her biggest motivators. She proved them wrong through her accomplishments. Ultimately, she learned a hard but valuable lesson: "Nothing is fair." She believes success requires relentless effort, as nothing in life comes easily. Now retired, she enjoys traveling and reading, reflecting on her journey and the progress she has witnessed. One of her proudest historical moments was Kamala Harris running for president, representing progress for women of color. "This was an important moment in our country's history," said Mosley. "Never let anyone discourage you and know who you are. No one can change who you are. You shouldn't let anyone make you be someone you aren't. Know who you are and decide based on what you know what you want to be!"

Dr. Mosley's attributes exude perseverance, strength, and determination that can break even the toughest barriers. She knew what her goals were and knew what she wanted to do. Despite facing inequality and personal hardships, she never let adversity define her. Dr. Mosley's dedication to the medical field, leadership roles, and commitment to empowering others, especially women of color, serve as a source of inspiration. Dr. Mosley's story reminds us that true strength resides in never allowing challenges to diminish your potential!

Major Achievements

- Overcoming homelessness during the aftermath of Hurricane Katrina
- Baptist Health Corporate Board Member
- Court Appointed Special Advocate
- Girls Incorporated of Fort Smith
- President of Chi Eta Phi Sorority
- Epsilon Nu Chapter of Sigma Theta Tau International Honor Society for Nurses

Mayor George B. McGill – City of Fort Smith, Arkansas

In the heart of Fort Smith, Arkansas, a young boy born during the era of segregation would one day rise to become a symbol of progress and leadership in his community. That young boy was George B. McGill, a man whose journey from humble beginnings to becoming the first Black Mayor of Fort Smith, Arkansas is a testament to perseverance, service, and the power of change.

Born on August 22, 1946, McGill grew up in a world where racial barriers were deeply entrenched, yet he never allowed those obstacles to define his future. Instead, he dedicated his life to public service, and education, advocating for a better future for all. Mayor McGill's roots run deep in Fort Smith, where he was raised in a caring, safe, and giving community. He recalls a childhood filled with happiness, where the community looked out for one another, and kindness was a way of life.

He attended Dunbar Elementary School where all grade levels were taught in a single classroom. He developed a strong sense of discipline and curiosity. Due to this, he was able to hear all the lessons that were taught. "By the time I got to the third grade, I knew it by heart!" said Mayor McGill. His fond memories of playing

By Kassidy Badger - tenth- grade scholar at Northside High School, and Mayor George B. McGill

baseball, climbing trees, and games like "Red Light, Green Light" reflect the simple joys of his upbringing. "Even though it was during a time of segregation, my fond memories are centered around the fact that we had lived in a great community," Mayor McGill recalled. "My life was full of fun as a kid."

Though McGill's commitment to his community extends far beyond politics, he plays an active role in numerous organizations, including the Fort Smith Round Table, the Symphony Board, the Fort Smith Boys & Girls Club, the Board of Education, the Fort Smith International Film Festival, and the National Association for the Advancement of Colored People (NAACP). Despite his successful career in finance, McGill's calling to serve extended beyond business. He spent thirty years in personal finance, eventually retiring from McGill Financial Services. His expertise and leadership led him to serve in the Arkansas House of Representatives District 78, and on the City of Fort Smith's Planning Commission, where he worked hard to create positive change. When asked to run for the position of Mayor, a role he had not sought, his sense of duty compelled him to step forward. His dedication is evident in every position he holds, always striving to better the lives of those around him.

Serving his community has been both an honor and a privilege. Though his leadership has brought great fulfillment, it has also come

Arkansas State Capitol Building

with challenges, proving that public service is not as easy as it may seem. One of his notable accomplishments was his work to separate the Martin Luther King Jr. holiday from President Robert E. Lee's, a change that removed confusion and acknowledged the significance of Dr. King's legacy. His leadership was never about seeking approval; it was about doing what was right. He asked, "At the end of the day, is it valuable to you?" This is a guiding principle that helped him stay true to his purpose despite adversity.

Of all his achievements, McGill considers his greatest accomplishments to be earning the title of Mayor, making his family proud, and seeing the results of his hard work. Beyond his professional successes, he measures his legacy by the impact he has made upon others. He spends his time helping people, traveling, and mentoring future leaders. His philosophy is grounded in the lessons he has learned over the years: "Be a good person, do not yield to negative thoughts, learn to forgive, and always be kind. Have the courage to do what's right, even if it seems as if it doesn't matter," he advises. He believes in never giving up on people, raising the bar, and striving for self-improvement every day. "No one is perfect," he acknowledges, "but we can all be rich in kindness." Through his work in government, business, and community service, Mayor George B. McGill has built a legacy of resilience, generosity, and unwavering commitment to others. His

Mayor McGill honored Captain Josh Edwards, Fort Smith Fire Department, with the Spirit of Service award during the Annual State of the City Address on March 18, 2025 (Photograph courtesy of the City of Fort Smith)

story serves as a powerful reminder that true leadership is not about titles or recognition. It is about making a lasting difference in the lives of people and raising the standards of excellence for future generations!

Major Achievements

- Bachelor of Science in Education from the University of Arkansas

- Master of Business Administration from the University of Arkansas

- Commissioned as Second Lieutenant, United States Army Field Artillery, during the Vietnam War era.

- Elected Mayor of Fort Smith August 2019 - present

- State Representative of District 78

  - Youth Legislative & Military Affairs Committee and Co-Chair of Policy-Making Subcommittee for the Legislative Governing Board of the Council of State Governments.

- United States Army Veteran

- Former business owner

Works Cited

Raya, Daisy. "Kassidy Badger and Mr. George McGill Interview Image." 25 Jan. 2025. Accessed 25 Jan. 2025.

"Annual State of the City Address." *City of Fort Smith, Arkansas's Facebook Page,* 18 Mar.2025, www.facebook.com/story.php?storyfbid=1062145215942268&id=10 0064403993494&rdr. Accessed 19 March 2025.

"Arkansas State Capital Building." *National Institute of Standards and Technology (NIST),* 3 Oct. 2017, www.nist.gov/image/arkansas-state-capitol-front-flags-golden-doors-domejpg. Accessed 19 March 2025.

Chief Danny Baker – Fort Smith Police Department

Looking through another set of lenses allows us to see beyond what our own perceived reality was once. Exploring and understanding unfamiliar perspectives and worldviews helps us find empathy and compassion where there was once judgment in a world full of inherently good people who are just lost or have simply taken a wrong turn. This is a dominant rule Chief Danny Baker lives by.

Chief Danny Baker, Fort Smith Police Department, demonstrates compassion as he goes the extra mile beyond just being a typical chief of a police department. He is certainly not a typical law enforcement official by any means. He views his professional and personal experiences through multiple lenses. He embodies this idea, proving that sometimes the most powerful change happens when you choose to see and understand the person behind the mistakes. He acknowledges that people are not defined by their mistakes but by their ability to grow from them. His resolve is to make a positive impact, whether it changes the outcome or not, which makes him a true leader.

By Jason Peraza - tenth-grade scholar at Northside High School

Chief Baker was born in the small city of McAlester, Oklahoma, in 1973. He and his wife Becky have been married twenty-eight years, raising four children of their own and adopting their fifth child from foster care in November 2019. They are all cherished equally. His wife, Becky, teaches Biological Science at a middle school and often has entertaining stories to share about her day.

Baker acknowledges his parents as his first and most important influences, shaping him into the strong person he is today. They instilled a strong work ethic in him, which he carries today. Though he knows it was disappointing to see him go the errant path early on, he points out "My parents were there for me and have always supported and believed in me." In his early thirties, he met the most influential person from his adult life, Don Cherry, a Black minister who became his closest friend and mentor during a difficult time in his church. His arrival sent shockwaves through the predominantly white congergation. Despite the tension, the two became incredibly close. Their daily conversations helped him work through struggles, both personal and professional. He describes Don Cherry as not just a constant sounding board but as someone who gave him perspective, helping him see life, policing, and people through a different lens. "I really learned to appreciate and embrace that, and Don Cherry did that for me. I'll be forever grateful for our friendship and his presence in my life."

In 1991, Baker graduated from Poteau High School in Oklahoma with honors, and he had many scholarship offers. Right out of high school, Baker enrolled at Oklahoma State University in Stillwater. He pursued a major in Criminal Justice and a minor in Psychology. Like many first-time college students, he embraced his new freedom, prioritizing fun, and a social life over academics. This was a decision he later admitted "came at a cost," recognizing that his choices affected his studies. Realizing he needed a way to support himself and stay in school, he decided to join the military. He served for eight years in the United States Army Reserve and Army National Guard while furthering his education. This experience helped him cover the costs of school. He values his military service and the extensive training that came along with it. "It provided the discipline I needed at that point in my life," said Baker. "It was a catalyst that pushed me to get past the partying and having a good time. It made me realize there's a serious world out there, and I had to take things more seriously." He returned to Poteau to Carl Albert State College and worked hard to improve his grade-point average. Later, Baker transferred to Northeastern State University in Tahlequah, Oklahoma, earning an associate degree in psychology and a bachelor's degree in criminal justice.

Baker got married while still in college and landed his first law enforcement job at the Mayes County sheriff's office, in Pryor, Oklahoma shortly after graduating. He has fond memories of his time at Northeastern State University, acknowledging many instructors and classmates for pushing him to think more critically and outside the box about policing, and how law enforcement should be about interacting with the public they serve. Chief Baker acknowledged, "There were a lot of seeds planted in me then that made me develop later in my career. You never know what information and what knowledge that you're gleaning that may not seem relevant today, but those seeds could take root and sprout twenty years later."

In 2015, after seeing news of yet another Black man killed by police, Baker, eighteen years into his career as a policeman, began questioning what was going wrong. He thought to himself, *"Maybe I need to start looking through another set of lenses, maybe I need to start viewing things from a different perspective."* He realized he couldn't find answers by talking to people who looked and thought like him. He prayed, asking God to show him how he could help fix the disconnect. Little did he know that prayer marked the beginning of a journey he never expected, one that would lead him to the Chief's Office in the end. He wasn't asking to become Chief, but after a series of events, including the resignation of the Chief at the time over a racist remark and the hiring of Fort Smith's first Black police chief, Baker found himself learning from new perspectives. He confronted his own biases, realizing his worldview wasn't the only one. This shifted his mindset, he began to see his job as not just as enforcing laws, but as being a guardian and caretaker for the community. He knew officers needed to do better, treat people better, and pursue peace with more intention.

Baker's career spans over twenty-seven years, with twenty-four of them dedicated to the Fort Smith Police Department. where he now serves as Chief. His path wasn't always easy. Early on, he worked side jobs as a self-taught carpenter, doing finish work and cabinet work to make ends meet. Before that, he held various jobs in college, from working fast food to being a resident assistant. His first law enforcement job was with the Mayes County Sheriff's office in Pryor, Oklahoma, working as a dispatcher and jailer. He later became an officer in Heavener, Oklahoma, before joining the Fort Smith Police Department in 2001, where he's been ever since. In 2022, he secured an almost twenty-four percent, across-the-board, pay raise for all sworn officers except for himself, achieving the highest one-time pay increase in Fort Smith's history. Reflecting on his journey, he acknowledges the highs and lows of a job, but he firmly believes, "Being a police chief is more than a full-time job, but I believe very strongly in being involved with the community beyond just what you'd normally think of as a police officer's duties." Chief Baker often tells new recruits, "You're embarking on the noblest profession you could do because few other jobs allow you to impact people during their worst moments. The way you help someone through their crisis doesn't just affect them, it reaches far beyond them to their loved ones and their future." Those moments of impact, he says, "Are what keep him going, especially when former strangers come back years later to tell him if it hadn't been for him, their life would have taken a completely different path." In 2022, he was selected the Outstanding Chief of Police by the Arkansas Fraternal Order of Police and received the 2023 Community Service Award from the Fort Smith Roundtable.

Over time, Baker's understanding of policing evolved. He once viewed the job as black and white, right or wrong, legal or not legal, but experience reshaped that mindset. "The law is black and white," he explains, "but life isn't. There's a whole lot of gray areas we can operate in." He no longer refers to himself and his officers as "law enforcement" because it feels too narrow. "Law enforcement is easy; it doesn't require much investment in people. Policing, though, is about more than arresting people. It's about figuring out what's causing the problem and connecting people to the right resources, whether that's therapy, mental health support, or something else. Jail isn't always the answer, it's not designed to fix people, it just gets them out of the public eye for a while." He reflects on the disconnect between society and policing, saying, "We've always wanted to take the low-hanging fruit and say we're just law enforcement, and every problem is a nail and we're the hammer, but society expects more than that." He believes that if you can spend a little more time investing in someone, in finding the actual root of the problem and connecting them to the correct resources, that's the better path. Baker explains, "Some people need to go to jail, but a lot of times, jail isn't the best option." He has been instrumental in changing Arkansas State law to allow for sobering facilities as an alternative to incarceration and further permitting officers to remotely book misdemeanor offenders at a detention facility instead of arresting them. The Fort Smith Police Department has significantly reduced the incarceration rate while continuing to effectively control crime under Baker's leadership.

Baker recognized the department lacked a clear direction, leading him to create a vision statement to guide their mission. He asked himself, *"How am I going to change what I see happening around me?"* and from that, the S.H.I.E.L.D. (Service, Honor, Integrity, Education, Legacy, Dedication) philosophy was born. The goal is to seek permanent peace and security for everyone. He emphasizes that they are "trying to work ourselves out of a job by pursuing perfection,  knowing that excellence will come from that pursuit, and seeing every encounter as an opportunity to improve, both for the officer and the person they're interacting with." The vision ensures that every action, policy, and decision has purpose and meaning.

Outside of his demanding, 24/7 role as Chief, Baker stays deeply involved in his church and in the community. He attends West Ark Church of Christ in Fort Smith, where he serves as a fill-in worship leader and sings bass on the praise team, focusing on gospel and acapella music as part of a project called Praise and Harmony. Previously, he was a full-time worship leader before moving to Fort Smith. When he's not working, he cherishes every moment spent with his kids and grandkids and he also enjoys hands-on projects, especially working on his over one-hundred-year-old house, saying, "There's always something to improve." He also likes target shooting with his son and dad, attending local civic events, and reading leadership books, particularly those by his favorite author, John Maxwell.

Baker believes that justice and mercy can coexist. He understands that most people are not truly bad people, but rather, they've made poor decisions. Baker's focus is on guiding people away from those mistakes or helping them get back on track, knowing this approach creates a safer community rather than simply locking people up. He values the idea that "everybody has value in the eyes of God, and they may just need the right opportunity to succeed." He also lives by the principle that leadership isn't about self-promotion, but about lifting others up. "If something good is to be said about you, it needs to be said by somebody else." Even when public opinion goes the other way, he refuses to engage with negativity on social media, saying, "If I do the right thing, somebody else is gonna tell the story, I don't have to." Resisting that urge for self-promotion, he says, is one of the biggest lessons he's learned. For him, resisting self-promotion and doing the right thing is the key to true leadership.

Major Achievements

- Graduated in 2018 from The Criminal Justice Institute Police Chief Executive Development Course at The University of Arkansas.

- In September 2019, he was selected as the department's Chief of Police after a nationwide search and is one of the first chiefs to be promoted from within the ranks of Fort Smiith Police Department (FSPD) in over thirty years.

- Led the department's very successful response to the historic Arkansas River flood of 2019.

- Graduated in 2021 from the International Police Executive Research Forum, from their Senior Management Institute for Police.

- Served in the United States Army Reserve and Arkansas Army National Guard for eight years.

- Served in multiple roles within the Fort Smith Police Department— Patrol, Field Training Officer, SWAT, Detective, Vice/Narcotics Supervisor, Special Operations Captain, Deputy Chief of Patrol, and Interim Chief.

- 2022 graduate of FBI's Law Enforcement Executive Development Seminar.

- Currently holds a Chief Level II certification with Arkansas Standards.

- Developed a new vision statement for the FSPD.

- Implementation of the first true co-response Crisis Intervention unit (CIU) in the state, a pre-arrest diversion program for non-violent, misdemeanor offenders, and the creation of a Vulnerable Persons Database to aid in the quick recovery of lost/missing people.

- Currently serves on the following state and local boards— Arkansas State 911 Board (second term), Hamilton Center for Child Advocacy, Fort Smith Health Advisory Council, the Fort Smith Museum of History (Vice President), and the Christmas Honors program.

- He is a life member of the Sebastian County Branch of the NAACP.

Works Cited

Baker, Chief Danny. "Fort Smith Police Department's Vision." *Fort Smith Police Department*,
www.fortsmithar.gov/government/departments/police. Accessed 23 Mar. 2025.

Mrs. Dorothy Johnson– Woman of Distinction

    In today's world, everyone is equal under the law and entitled to all the same civil rights. That said, this was not the case for Mrs. Dorothy J. Sanders-Johnson, who was born in 1932 and raised in the South during the Jim Crow era of American History. In the face of discrimination and segregation, however, Mrs. Johnson dedicated her life to serving and helping others. Throughout her long and fruitful life, she had many roles: former Director of the Monitoring and Equal Employment Departments under the Western Arkansas Employment Development agency, former President of the National Association of Colored Women's Clubs (NACWC) of Arkansas, current President of the Phillis Wheatley Women's Club, Mother, Grandmother, Wife, and more. Mrs. Johnson, a person of strong and resilient character, represents the very best of us. She cannot be defined under any singular title; instead, Mrs. Johnson should be remembered for her influence in the community around her, the path she has forged, and the history she has made.

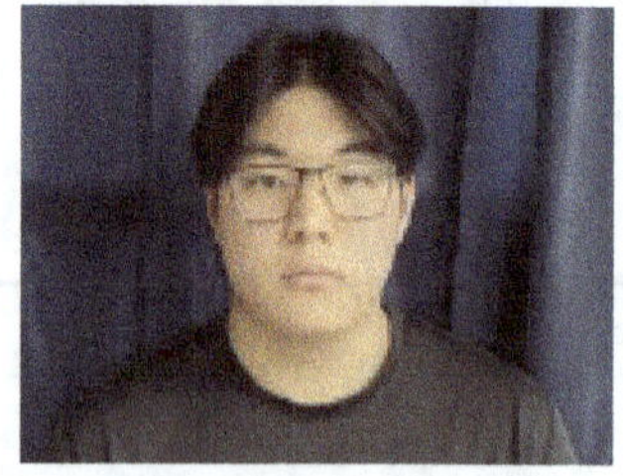

By Josh Chung – eleventh-grade scholar at Southside High School

Mrs. Dorothy J. Sanders-Johnson was born and raised in Alma, Arkansas. Today, much of Arkansas has urbanized, but back then, as Mrs. Johnson described Alma as "a small rural town." She grew up in the household of her great-grandmother, a former slave, where she lived alongside her immediate and extended family. In her early life, Mrs. Johnson went to a segregated school that was a two-room building, one classroom for first through sixth grades and the other for seventh through twelfth grades, where she was taught by her aunt. When asked to describe the differences between the black and white schools, she said, "The other schools had buses, they had a nice building and new books... they had everything they needed–unfortunately, all they allowed for us was a two-room building and we got their used books." Just to get to school every day, Mrs. Johnson had to walk more than four miles. After eighth grade, she attended Lincoln High School in Fort Smith because the segregated high schools in Alma and Van Buren had closed. Mrs. Johnson's experience was very common for black high school students in the area: students who lived even as far away as Fayetteville (a little over an hour's drive) attended Lincoln High School. After graduating from high school, she was unable to attend college because Fort Smith Junior College (today known as the University of Arkansas - Fort Smith) did not allow black students, and she did not have the resources to attend school elsewhere. So, instead of going to college, Mrs. Johnson decided to settle down after meeting and marrying her late husband, Rev. James B. Johnson, with whom she has two children.

For many people, starting a family and finding a stable job is where they stop, but Mrs. Johnson did not stop. Even though she did not go to college after high school, in later years, when federally funded educational training programs became available, she attended classes at Westark College, now UAFS. Mrs. Johnson never stopped learning. After high school, she worked at a department store for about thirteen years. When asked why she decided to work there for so long, Mrs. Johnson said that many people would characterize her job as "menial", but for her, this job was an opportunity to learn. Furthermore, she said that it was because of the way she was raised: which was to "make the best out of every situation." As a result, Mrs. Johnson learned how to do many of the jobs in the store so well that she was the person that they came to whenever they needed someone to fill in for a job. Despite being qualified to work at higher-paying positions in the department store, those jobs were not available to people of color. As a black woman, there were opportunities that she never got and barriers she had to face, and Mrs. Johnson overcame those barriers, always making the best of her situation. This can especially be seen after she left her job at the department store and completed Westark Business classes. She was hired as a secretary for the Neighborhood Youth Corps, a federally funded youth employment training program that provided work experience during the summer and after school for area students. After several years, when adult employment in the area was impacted by the closing of Whirlpool, the training programs were expanded to include adults. Crawford-Sebastian Community Development Agency and the Western Arkansas Employment Development Agency were designated

Dorothy Johnson & Janis F. Kearney

agencies managing these programs. She worked there for thirty-one years, working her way up from secretary to being Director of Monitoring and Director of Equal Employment Opportunity. At the same time, she was very involved in the civic and social activities in the community.

Mrs. Johnson was elected president of the NACWC Southwest Region (seven states), a recognized national organization empowering women and youth (girls and boys) working together to improve the standards of the home and community through service and advocacy. In the late 1980s to mid-1990s, she was the primary organizer of the Martin Luther King, Jr. Planning Committee She served as the chairperson for eight years. where she was responsible for coordinating various events surrounding the honoring and furthering of Reverend Doctor Martin Luther King, Jr. and his ideals, including youth activities, an awards banquet, community ecumenical services, a parade, and a scholarship program.

In the early 2000s, the NACWC of Arkansas received the NACWC Outstanding State Award because of her work coordinating disaster relief for those affected by Hurricane Katrina. Today, Mrs. Johnson serves as the president of the NACWC of Arkansas' Phillis Wheatley Federated Club of Ft. Smith. She is an advisor to the Phillis Wheatley Girls Club, where she assists young girls, guiding them on their path toward a successful future. The Phillis Wheatley Club is one of the oldest clubs in the NACWC, founded in 1898 and has been active continuously for over one hundred twenty-five years.

Mrs. Johnson is an active member of Unity Missionary Baptist Church, NAACP, Democratic Women, and Lincoln Alumni Association. She is a 1994 graduate of Leadership Ft. Smith, and in 2005, she was named a Woman of Distinction by the Girl Scouts Council, Mt. Magazine Area of Western Arkansas and Eastern Oklahoma. In January 2006, she received the Martin Luther King, Jr., Golden Hands Awards from Mayor McGill and Allstate Insurance Co. Additionally, Mrs. Johnson won the Martin Luther King, Jr. Achievement Award from the Martin Luther King, Jr Planning Committee for twenty years of continuous service. In 2007, she received the Ft. Smith Public Library Black Heritage Award and the Mayor's (Ray Baker) Appreciation Award and was also, selected one of the Twelve Leading Ladies of the Ft. Smith–Van Buren area by the Junior League. She has served on numerous Boards and Committees and served as the first secretary for Habitat for Humanity when it was formed. In 2022, Mrs. Johnson received the Lincoln High School Alumni Association Lifetime Achievement Award and the Making History Award from Ft. Smith Mayor George McGill. She has also received other awards from her church and other civic groups.

After asking Mrs. Johnson why it is important to preserve history, this was her answer: "Having been born and raised in a small rural town during the era of segregation, and since there is little or no documented/recorded Black history, it is important that my children and grandchildren know my history. History provides an important link between what was, what is, and what is to be and explains why some things are the way they are now." Mrs. Johnson's life epitomizes that link, that history. By always making the best out of every situation she was given, she took hate, ignorance, and hardship and crafted it into equality, compassion, and success. Mrs. Johnson is a success story, but more than that, she represents hope—the hope of a mistreated people who, instead of turning to violence, turned to love." Her favorite quote is, "If we all join hands, we can reach twice as far."

Mrs. Judy Christian– Retired Teacher, Ramsey Junior High School

"Making a difference in the lives of my students as an educator was my greatest accomplishment, largely because I truly loved my work. Even now, former students and their parents tell me how much they enjoyed my class. It has been fourteen years since I retired from teaching, and I still hold those memories close to my heart!" ~Mrs. Judy Christian, an educator still influencing the next generation

Judy Christian was born in October 1948 at Twin City Hospital in Fort Smith, Arkansas. "I was married to Calvin Christian for thirty-six years." She is the proud mother of her son Spencer, and has four wonderful bonus children: Regina, Chris, Lori, and Nita. Mrs. Christian received her degree from Philander Smith College in Little Rock, Arkansas.

Though she never imagined she would become a teacher, as a child, she often "played" school and was always the teacher.

As a result, when she declared her major in college, it seemed only natural to pursue teaching. She went on to teach for forty-two years, thoroughly enjoying every year. Her first teaching

By Sage Hardie - eleventh-grade scholar at Northside High School

experience was in Jersey City, New Jersey. In Fort Smith she taught part time at Westark Community College and retired from Ramsey Junior High School after thirty-five years.

When asked about the person who had the greatest influence on her life, Mrs. Christian responded, "My youth pastor, Willie Lee Washington, was truly remarkable. She always made me feel special, and her care for me was sincere. She was the first person to encourage me to attend college and even took me to visit an Historically Black College and University (HBCU) campus affiliated with the United Methodist Church. After two visits to that campus, I knew I wanted to attend, and I did. Her determination continues to impact my life today, because of my college education."

Since retiring from teaching, Mrs. Christian holds leadership positions in five organizations. She serves as assistant treasurer for both the Fidelity Women's Club and Delta Sigma Theta Sorority, Inc. Additionally, she is the treasurer for the Northwest Region of Federated Clubs, and the Lincoln High School Alumni Association. Mrs. Christian also serves as the Chairperson of Pastor Parish Relations at Mission United Methodist Church. She said, "My favorite is my church position because it is not as demanding as the other organizations, and I love the rapport with my church members."

Mrs. Christian loves to travel and read. She said, "It's so relaxing!"

Mrs. Christian has sound advice for youth today. "It has often been said that today's youth live in a world numb to violence, accustomed to death, and surprised by nothing. However, do not let this reality diminish your zest for life.

As you journey through life, you will face challenges, and through these experiences, you will learn and grow. The world is full of opportunities—do not hesitate to pursue something that sparks your interest. Always remember, you have the power to make tomorrow a better place.

Set clear goals for your life, and devise a plan to achieve them, but also practice patience, as time is an essential factor in everything.

When you attend your first job interview, be punctual. Being late will not leave a good impression. Dress professionally—avoid wearing jeans, flip-flops, sweatshirts, or tank tops in a business interview.

During the interview, maintain good posture by sitting upright with your feet flat on the floor. Respond to questions clearly and confidently—speak loudly, avoid mumbling, do not chew gum, and articulate your words fully. Refrain from using words like "uh," "ain't," and no profanity. Do not smack your lips, with your mouth open in a thinking mode.

Remember the first law of nature is self-preservation. Make your mental, physical and spiritual well-being a priority. It is easy to overlook your health, but taking care of yourself matters.

Finally, stay intellectually curious – keep reading, listening and learning.

These points will certainly be an asset for you.

Awards Received

- Who's Who Among America's Teachers
- Distinguished Alumni Award from Lincoln High School
- Making History Award presented by the Mayor of Fort Smith
- Fiftieth year membership in Delta Sigma Theta Sorority
- Lincoln Echo Good Samaritan Award

Mrs. Trish Richardson – Executive Director, Washington Community & Cultural Center

"A dream doesn't become reality through magic; it takes sweat, determination, and hard work." ~Colin Powell

Mrs. Trish Richardson was born in September of 1957 in Fort Smith, Arkansas at Fort Chaffee. Her dad, Sgt. Tommy Robinson, served in the United States Army. Richardson has two children; both are boys ages thirty-seven and forty-seven. "I have a bonus son who is fifty-four and a bonus daughter who is forty-two. Richardson's family traveled a lot when she was a young girl. "I was at Fort Benning in Georgia, and I think my latter elementary years were in El Paso, Texas. He retired, so we moved back to the area. I am a product of Fort Smith Public Schools. I attended Kimmons Junior High and then Northside High School." Her first marriage was about ten years and her second marriage was eleven years. She and her husband Jimmie, whom she recently lost, share a blended family. "I have a bonus son who is fifty-four, and a bonus daughter who is forty-two.

"I have a bachelor's degree in Workforce Development with an emphasis in Human

By Shilah Elise Lechner – eleventh-grade scholar at Northside High School

Resources from the University of Arkansas. I have a master's degree in education in Lifelong Learning from the University of Arkansas," said Richardson. The most influential person in her life was her dad. "He instilled in us very early reasons that we should pursue an education. He didn't talk about it a lot. I don't know if he thought he couldn't afford to send us, even with him being in the military, it was quite expensive. He had five children. The other person would be myself. I'm very driven. I believe in myself. I kind of surprise myself in the leaps and bounds I can make in education and in helping others," Richardson stated.

Mrs. Richardson does not have a lot of free time, but there is something that she loves to do when there is an opportunity. "I love to read," she said, "I don't have a lot of time for it, but I love to read. I am the founder and executive director of the Washington Community &  Cultural Center that just opened in October 2024. My husband fell ill, so I had to put it on the backburner. The name itself comes from the Washington Elementary School in Fort Smith. My greatest desire was to purchase that building and turn it into the center, but that didn't happen. So, now I'm housed at 3600 North Albert Pike Avenue. It was formerly the Ray Baker Senior Citizen Activity Center. So, now it's known as the Washington Community & Cultural Center. I am really, really excited about this! I will leave Fort Smith Public Schools in May after seven years with them, and I had about thirteen years of employment in higher education with about a total of twenty-one years in education. I'm really excited about this, and I hope that I will be able to help the students I encounter."

Richardson's center is education centered. "I'm between Jeffrey's and Stephen's Boys & Girls Clubs. I have access to Morrison, Spradling, Sutton, and Sunnymede. Those are the elementary schools. I'm, also, near Kimmons Junior High School. There are enough students to serve on this side of town. I think our center will benefit our community," said Richardson. "My center is more on the academic side as opposed to the Boys & Girls Clubs that focus on sports. Arkansas is low in their reading scores, and I'm a specialist in reading. I hope that the students I meet will excel."

Mrs. Richardson's center will host a Summer Reading Camp this summer. "Once I become a full-time employee in May, I will focus on aging adults. I am certified to teach Chair Yoga. We have Zumba and Line Dancing classes beginning soon that will be for all ages. I'm excited about being a partner with Fort Smith Public Schools because they have some summer camps focused on middle schools, and I'm going to try to engage with third to fifth grades. I want the center to be a liaison between the university and the community and between Fort Smith Public Schools and the community. I'm not trying to duplicate anything that they are doing, but I want to enhance or supplement anything that they have. This way the community has a lot of options and resources available to them."

Mrs. Richardson began saving money for her community center out of her own pocket. "My grandchildren have been very instrumental in helping to get the building ready for the summer. I'll need a coordinator or staff person to work here in the office because I really want to be involved here in the community. So, it will be me, a full-time person, and I'll have someone taking care of the building. The staff will be very small starting out. I have applied for several grants I probably won't know more about until June or July. I do lease the building out. It's available for repasses and birthday parties, and things like that. The community needs that. Sometimes you need a place a little bit bigger than your home. I can help with that." Richardson's building can hold a maximum of one hundred twenty people. She is leasing the building from the city, but she has cared and accentuated it as much as possible. "I love the space, and I hope the students will find it to be a very safe space," Richardson explained.

The hours of her center are Tuesday through Thursday from 4:00 PM to 6:00 PM. "After spring break, I plan to keep the building open until 7:00 PM because of longer daylight hours," Richardson said. Lynette Thrower, a UAFS employee, will lead the Zumba classes and the proceeds benefit the backpack program.

Major Achievements

- Earned a bachelor's degree in Workforce Development.
- Earned a master's degree in education with an emphasis in Human Resources.
- An educator for over twenty-one years.
- Founding the Washington Community & Cultural Center.

Mrs. Angela Walton-Raji– Author, Admissions Specialist, Wife

Mrs. Angela Walton-Raji is a historian, genealogist, educator, and writer who has been nationally recognized for her research on Oklahoma Freedman—descendants of formerly enslaved black people amongst the five civilized tribes, and her intimate knowledge of Native American and African American history. The author of multiple books on the subject, Mrs. Angela, was asked numerous times by the Smithsonian and Dartmouth College to lecture on her research. She has also received countless genealogical awards and has even been to Capitol Hill as an activist for Oklahoma Freedmen, providing information about them. Based on her professional career alone, she has already earned the title of "History Maker," but there is more to Mrs. Angela than meets the eye. Despite growing up in a hateful and dark chapter of American history, her life has blossomed into a beacon of curiosity and passion. One of the most important lessons that she has learned and imparts to her students is that everyone has a story to tell, and this is Mrs. Angela's story.

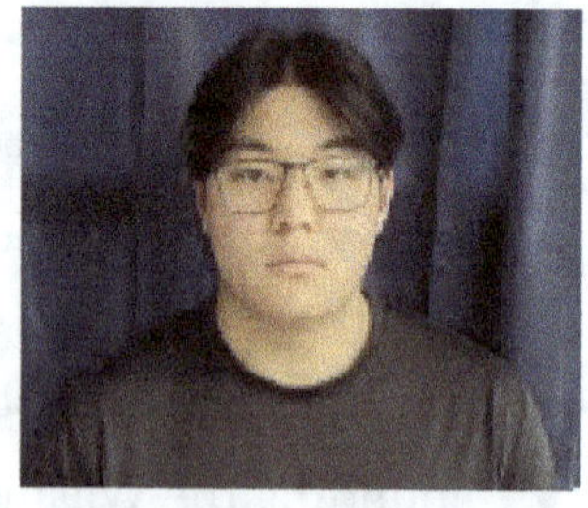

By Josh Chung – eleventh-grade scholar at Southside High School

Mrs. Angela Walton-Raji was born in Fort Smith, Arkansas, in 1951, at Twin City Hospital. Growing up in a catholic family, she attended St. John the Baptist Catholic School, St. Scholastica, and then graduated from St. Ann's Academy in 1969. Something important to notice is that Mrs. Angela grew up during a time when Fort Smith was segregated. She was born in a segregated hospital and went to segregated schools, most of the time. However, Mrs. Angela said that during those times, segregation never took away from the strength and interconnectedness of the black community; it only fed into it. She elaborated by reminiscing about her childhood spent at church socials, worshiping together and eating together, adding that her community was a close-knit one, assisting one another in times of need. Mrs. Angela further admitted that although segregation did take away some privileges, ultimately it did not hinder the progress and success of her community: "... being segregated didn't keep anyone who had ambition or desire from doing things." Her life is a testament to this as she continued her education at St. Louis University, where she earned a degree in Spanish, and later, a Master of Education from Antioch University. For many years after that, Mrs. Angela served as a college admissions specialist for Tufts, Boston University, and the University of Maryland, Baltimore County.

Mrs. Angela Walton-Raji had multiple jobs over her lifetime, and the one that brought her the most joy is her genealogy/writing career. While being an avid reader and aspiring to be an author since childhood, her professional career as a writer and genealogist did not take off until the 1990s after she met Dr. Agnes K. Callum, whom she credits as her source of inspiration and the spark of her career.

Around 1990 at a genealogy convention presented by Dr. Callum, Mrs. Angela remembered how someone in the audience that day had asked if Dr. Callum would write about and research civil war soldiers from Norfolk, Virginia. She remembers Dr. Callum answering that audience member "no" and explaining that they should let Norfolk people write about that. This was her "aha!" moment. Instead of letting herself think "Wow, this is really cool, I wish someone would write about Oklahoma and Arkansas," Mrs. Angela decided, "Wow, this really interests me, and I am going to write about the people and history of my hometown." A year later, Mrs. Angela uncovered her family's records about Oklahoma Freedmen and the records of twenty thousand freedmen from the Oklahoma and Western Arkansas area. She then went on to write multiple books and give numerous lectures on her research.

Today, Mrs. Angela is officially retired, but she never stopped writing. She continues to write and research for books that she has in progress. Furthermore, she blogs and has a podcast where she shares genealogical information. Mrs. Angela said that she technically never retired. She never stopped writing because she loves it and never saw it as work.

Nowadays, Mrs. Angela resides in Maryland with her husband, Ganiyu Raji, whom she has been married to for forty-five years. Though she has had no children of her own, she continues to maintain close relationships with her past students, nephews, and nieces. When she is not writing, researching, or blogging, Mrs. Angela says she likes to dabble in her garden and travel around when she can. She makes it a point to travel home to Fort Smith to visit her family.

Mrs. Cosaundra Chapple – Author, Playwright and Director

How many ordinary people take what they love to do, and make a production out of it? Not many, but that is exactly what Mrs. Cosaundra Chapple did with her love for writing and directing plays. This makes her extraordinary!

Mrs. Cosaundra Chapple was born on May 5, 1964, to Leroy and Louella Lewis, in the small, rural city of Cotton Plant, Arkansas. Chapple was raised in Brinkley, Arkansas with her four siblings. She has two sons—Christopher, Jr. and Tyrin. Chris Jr., thirty-six, graduated with a bachelor's degree in criminal justice from the University of Arkansas - Fort Smith (UAFS) in 2006. Tyrin, thirty, earned his high school diploma in 2023. Chapple instilled in her two sons the importance of education.

Mrs. Chapple graduated from Cotton Plant High School in 1982. "As a child, I liked going to school because I lived in the country and enjoyed

By Aiden Pope - tenth-grade scholar at Northside High School

being around the other kids. My favorite subject was English, and my least favorite was math," said Mrs. Chapple. She has been married for the past forty-two years to Christopher Chapple Sr., a minister and a custodian for Fort Smith Public Schools. Chapple began exploring her creative skills by writing and featuring plays at her church a decade ago. She attended UAFS and graduated in 2015 with a major in Theatre Arts and a minor in Speech. "I applied myself more in college," she stated.

According to Chapple, Mr. James Hamilton was one of the most influential people in her life. "He was my math teacher during my youth," said Chapple. "He always emphasized the importance of me showing my work. I'm a first-generation college graduate in my family, and this motivated me to push through and finish college strong. Finishing college has been one of my life's greatest accomplishments!"

Chapple worked as a cashier at Coleman's Pharmacy (2001 – 2009). She has been a self-employed, personal caregiver for two years. Her identity as a Christian has influenced her career choices. She utilizes her gift of compassion to pore into the lives of others through caregiving or by teaching life lessons through writing and producing plays.

During her leisure time, she enjoys doing arts and crafts. "I love to watch movies whether they be suspenseful or mystery. I listen to old-school music during my free time," Chapple reveals. She is a member of The Housewives of Fort Smith, a Christian women's charitable organization that seeks ways to give back to the community and those in need. Chapple has routinely volunteered at the Food Bank in the past. She enjoys reading and writing children's books. One of her books is titled *Dogs Are Bullied Too*. This book was written about her dog, Sebastian. Also, she is considering writing a memoir about her life.

"I write educational, realistic, and comedic plays," stated Chapple. Her most recent play, *Living on Grandma's Prayers*, was featured in 2023 at the King Opry House in Van Buren, Arkansas. Before this, Chapple's play *The Roommate* was featured at the King Opry House in 2017. "This play is about four women on fixed incomes living together to survive their economic circumstances. There is a lot of drama and comedy among these characters." *I Want'sa Be Free* was written in 2008 and revised by Chapple in 2016. She featured the play, *I Want'sa Be Free*, at the Van Buren Fine Arts Center on August 27, 2016. The play depicts life on a slave plantation during the 1800s. *Oh Lordy, What a Child!* was written by Chapple in 2010. The main lessons in this play are that nothing in life comes easy, and sometimes trial and error are the best means to help us grow. Cosaundra Chapple's talents as a writer and director add depth to the unique tapestry of Fort Smith!

Photograph courtesy of Mrs. Cosaundra Chapple

(Flyer courtesy of Mrs. Cosaundra Chapple)

Major Achievements

- First generation college graduate in her family.

- Chosen as a 2014 Unsung Hero at the University of Arkansas - Fort Smith.

- Plays: *O' Lordy What a Child* (2010); *I Want'sa Be Free* (2008 / 2016); *The Roommate* (2017); *Living on Grandma's Prayers* (2013)

- *Dogs Are Bullied Too* (2024)

Mrs. Sharon "Butterfly" Thomas Ray – Director, Actress, Producer and Programmer

Do you live a free, full, and "CRAZY" life? There is a woman known for living this way. She is courageous, bold, unique, fun-loving, supportive, and free-minded: A true hero in disguise. That person is Mrs. Sharon Thomas Ray and this is her story!

Mrs. Sharon Thomas Ray was born in 1948 in Little Rock, Arkansas. She and her husband, Oscar Dean Ray, Sr., have a blended family of seven children, twenty-eight grandchildren, and twelve great-grandchildren. Ray graduated from high school at age sixteen. Throughout her various jobs—including selling papers, tutoring, teaching, sales, and educational administration—she gained experience that led to her ultimate roles as an entrepreneur and professional volunteer. Mrs. Ray earned a master's degree in education from Pepperdine University. Also, Ray earned a bachelor's degree in behavioral sciences from California State University. While she worked and attended college, she realized she did not like working in low-status positions for a low income. "I always worked fast and finished first but always got paid less since the pay was

By Alexa Thibodeaux - tenth-grade scholar at Northside High School

hourly," said Ray. With her fast-working skills in many capacities, the hourly pay was not fair in her view. It was Mrs. Sharon Thomas Ray's rapid and neat working skills for less pay versus her coworkers' slow and messy skills for higher pay that made her wonder, *"Who is actually winning?"*

Mrs. Sharon Thomas Ray created a nickname for herself, due to her strong sense of self-awareness, and because she could do so. She became known as "Shiron Butterfly." This is a figurative symbol of Ray's freedom and strength in life. Ray went from working for people to working for herself, and she decided to do what she loved the most.

Mrs. Ray has over thirty years of training and experience in the motion picture industry. She has worked on more than twenty productions as a producer, casting director, production manager, sounder supervisor, production designer, make-up artist, and sound effects artist. She has even worked as a marketing and public relations consultant. Ray's goal is to create innovative methods to educate, motivate, and train the next generations of filmmakers, actors, directors, and crew.

Thirty-third Year Anniversary Muskogee Legacy Keeping

Ray founded Legacykeepersrus in 1991. She directs, produces, programs, and features original films. Ray teaches actors, film crews, and cinema. She has hosted numerous film and art festivals. Ray is devoted to cemetery preservation and restoration—a mission to identify, to get signage, to recruit caretakers, and to educate youth and adults about historical significance. According to Ray, "Tuskegee Airman, Faythe McGinnis, was the first Airman killed during flight exercises for the first training class graduation (with his mother in attendance). Cuba Gooding, Jr. was an actor featured in the HBO television movie titled *The Tuskegee Airmen* (1995) which filmed in Muskogee, Oklahoma and Fort Smith, Arkansas. At the time, we did not know about the airmen buried in the cemetery. Airman Robert Smith returned to Muskogee, became a physician, and died in 1992. Many other Tuskegee Airmen survived longer."

Actor, Cuba Gooding, Jr. visits Booker T. Washington Cemetery in Muskogee, Oklahoma

Ray volunteers at shelters, and advocates for those affected by domestic violence and women's health to bring awareness to these important issues. She is the structural finder of many people in so many ways. Everything she does has value in her life and creates value in the lives of others. "You can call me a pro- volunteer! Ha ha, I guess." She has been the host of the "Bare Bones International Film and Arts Festivals" for twenty-five years, and many more to come. The festival is where musicians, artists, actors, and film come together. "Oscar and I have been archiving video footage and interviews of blues musicians for the last twenty-three years during the "Dusk till Dawn Blues Festival" held each Labor Day in the tiny town of Rentiesville, Oklahoma," said Ray.

Bare Bones International Film & Music Festival (Founded 1999)

Ray would not have made it to where she is today had it not been for Zig Ziglar and Ms. Roundtree, whom she considers having had the "most influence" upon her career and life. "If there was no Zig Ziglar, there probably would be no me," Ray said affectionately. Growing up listening to and watching his tapes, Ziglar became her structure. Ziglar is the reason why she created her nickname "Shiron Butterfly."

A second influential force in Ray's life was Ms. Roundtree. "She became my everything. My inspiration to become a schoolteacher came from her influence." Ms. Roundtree was Ray's first-grade teacher in the Little Rock School District. Ray found her true self from Ms. Roundtree's nurturing presence in her life. "Ms. Roundtree taught me to help people, to be non-judgmental, and to keep balance in an already messed up world. She would say 'In order to succeed, you must help someone else succeed,'" Ray said.

When Ray has a break, she watches movies to learn something new for her class, listens to Blues music, and overall does everything she can to create something new. "Some people say I work a lot and never rest. Which I cannot disagree with," stated Ray. "I'm always teaching. Always teaching!" There are no breaks for this hardworking and dedicated woman which has made her the success story that she is today.

Mrs. Ray's philosophy for leading a good life is "To do well in life, do what you love, take time for others, make others matter, and be yourself. Remember to stay in control; but be open-minded. Do what you love! Do more than you are asked! Volunteer! Get out into the world, stay fun and creative." Mrs. Ray stated, "Life is what you make it!"

Major Achievements

- The lessons that her children have learned and taught her.
- Acted in more than nine independent movies/films.
- New board member of the Circle Cinema and Arthouse Theater in Tulsa, Oklahoma
- Member of the Oklahoma Motion Picture Alliance
- Member of Women in Safe Home
- Muskogee Tourism Authority Trustee
- Inducted into the Oklahoma Movie Hall of Fame
- Listed in Who's Who in America
- Received a Special Recognition Award from the 2005 Oklahoma Governor Arts Award
- Muskogee Area Arts Council
- Member of Rotary International
- Member of the Association of Film and Video Professionals, Women in Film
- Member of Wild Geese Alliance of Independent Film Producers
- Mid-America Association of Film Festival Directors
- Oklahoma Music Hall of Fame
- Filmmakers Against Child Abuse
- Preventing Abuse In Neighborhoods (P.A.I.N.) Foundation
- Women of Vision, Female Filmmakers of Oklahoma, Camera Gurlz, Muskogee Area Film Production Ambassadors
- Member of the National Association of the Advancement of Colored People (NAACP)

Works Cited

Spaulding, C. (2023). Cuba Gooding Jr. Visits Muskogee [Photograph]. *Muskogee Phoenix.* https://www.muskogeephoenix.com/news/cuba-gooding-jr-visits- muskogee/articleb661dc82-8eba-11ed-8d0e-23529a7c5fbb.html

Thirty-Third Anniversary Legacy Keeping in Muskogee, Oklahoma [Photograph]. *Legacy Keepers Preserving History One Story at A Time.* https://barebonesfilmfest00.tripod.com/legacykeepersrus/id71.html

Thomas-Ray, S. (2025). Welcome To Muskogee OK! USA [Photograph]. Bare Bones International Film & Music Festival. https://barebonesfilmfest00.tripod.com/index.html

Ms. Cathy Triplett – Entrepreneur & Owner of Ebony Hair Images Hair Salon

"Life is more beautiful when you meet the right hairdresser," Peter Coppola, a famous hair stylist, salon owner, and businessman.

The best hair stylists maintain longevity, not only for their skills in hair care but also for their skills in caring about people. Ms. Cathy Triplett was born in Fort Smith, Arkansas in January 1961. She has two daughters, two sons, and six grandchildren. "I became a foster parent to my great-nephew when he was two days old for eleven years," said Triplett. She has been the proprietor of Ebony Hair Images Hair Salon for over forty years.

By Roxy Logan - eleventh-grade scholar at Northside High School

Triplett moved to Massachusetts after she graduated from Northside High School in 1979, and she attended the John Powers Modeling School in Massachusetts. "Once I returned to Fort Smith, I began giving fashion and hair shows. I taught participants how to walk and pivot. It was a lot of fun. I like to put smiles on peoples' faces," Triplett said. "I've done creative collaborations with other hair stylists."

Triplett earned an associate degree at Carl Albert State College in Poteau, Oklahoma in 2010. "I earned a bachelor's degree in professional organizational leadership in 2021 at Arkansas Tech University, Russellville, Arkansas, noted Triplett. After being in business for forty years, Triplett can attest to life being more than what

you do for a living. "Now, I work part-time at my salon and take care of my great-nephew. I have heard a lot of sadness and joy while communicating with my clients in my salon over the years. They can trust me with whatever they are going through which is more important than getting their hair styled. It is about caring for others. Whatever is said in my salon, remains in my salon," Triplett stated.

Ms. Cathy Triplett - 2021 Commencement Ceremony at Arkansas Tech University, Russellville, Arkansas

Triplett worked at a preschool that serves children with developmental disabilities for ten years after earning her associate degree. "I enjoy working with preschoolers, exercising with them, getting down on the floor with them at circle time, and teaching curriculum. The children are our future, and they need to be prepared for what the future holds," Triplett added.

Ms. Triplett has faced and overcame a significant challenge in her life. "I'm an eleven-year survivor of breast cancer. I have celebrated the life that God has given me every five years. God has blessed me to share blessings, and I know that He has left me here for a reason because I have known many people who did not make it, so I thank God that I'm eleven years free of cancer! To God be the glory in everything that I do. I just want to be used by Him!" Triplett declares.

Semi-retirement has not slowed Ms. Triplett down. "I like to read, sing, do yard work, and garden in my spare time," she said. "I have a missionary women's support group, and I like to volunteer at the Reynolds Support House, and I participate in book clubs," said Triplett. "I like to be used by God as much as possible."

Ms. Triplett has advice she would like to share with others who may be struggling. "Focus on your goals. Do not give up on your dreams! "The bible says to not worry about tomorrow (Matthew 6:34). Do not worry about things (Philippians 1:4-6). Let God take care of you.

Whatever your dream is in life, trust God with the steps to take," Triplett encourages. "Take one day at a time."

Ms. Cathy Triplett and her family (October 2024)

Tenth Year Cancer Free Dinner Celebration

Major Achievements

- Ms. Cathy Triplett's children and grandchildren are her greatest achievements.

- Cancer Survivor for eleven years

- Participating with a women's missionary group.

- The success of Ebony Hair Images Hair Salon for over forty years

- Earning a bachelor's in professional organization leadership at Arkansas Tech University, Russellville, Arkansas.

- Attended John Powers Modeling School in Massachusetts

- Volunteer at the Reynolds Cancer Support House

Mr. Bill Word –Retired Businessman & Volunteer

"There is a fountain of youth—it is your mind, your talents, the creativity you bring to your life and the lives of people you love. When you learn to tap this source, you will truly have defeated age," said Sophia Loren, actress.

Mr. Bill Word's life experiences are a testament to this famous quote. Now retired, life has not slowed down as he remains engaged with several organizations he serves.

Mr. Word was born on May 6, 1947, in Memphis, Tennessee, to Charles A. Word and Velma Milam Word. During the earlier part of his life, he lived a nomadic life with his mother after his parents divorced while he was in the first grade. He finally settled with his mother and stepfather in Frayser, Tennessee. He graduated from Frayser High School. Mr. Word continued his education at the Memphis State University for two and one-half years and soon got married. "I tried to work and carry twelve hours in night classes, but I found out that I could not do that after our first child was born. I often say that is when I transferred to the School

By Tarissa Thibodeaux - eleventh-grade scholar at Northside High School

71

of Hard Knocks. I dropped out with the plan to get things better organized and go back. I never did," Word revealed.

Later in life, Mr. Word began his adult business career with Lewis Supply Company at 477 South Main Street, Memphis, Tennessee. He was hired to work in the warehouse. "After a few years, I was promoted to work in the office as a buyer, interviewing factory salesmen, writing letters to customers and vendors," Mr. Word shared. A few years later, Word was offered a job as an inside salesman for Die Supplies, Inc. in Memphis, Tennessee. I accepted the job offer," Word fondly remembers. "After being transferred to Fort Smith, a customer asked me to join the Elks Lodge to get to meet people. I eventually became the Exalted Ruler of the Lodge for two terms. Our charity was the Children's Colony in Booneville. During my time as an office holder, we built an athletic field for them. We also donated some special shoes so that a young adult could walk. He had been dragging himself across the floor because he did not have the shoes. During that time, I was elected president of the Society of Manufacturing Engineers, even though I wasn't an Engineer. During that time, I was working for E.C. Blackstone, an industrial distributor, that had opened a branch in Fort Smith. They asked me to transfer to Jackson, Mississippi. I told them I couldn't until I completed my terms as a leader for the Elks Lodge and the Society of Manufacturing Engineers. They told me that I had thirty days to be in Jackson, or I should resign. I resigned. I learned that it's a lot more difficult to get a job when you don't have a job. After being out of work for three months, I was about to move back to Memphis when I got a call from Temple Supply—a plumbing supply and heating and air distributor that wanted to open an Industrial Supply Division. They wanted to hire me as their salesman. I gladly accepted their offer. I feel blessed to have been able to make Fort Smith my home."

Mr. Word had the opportunity to take a Dale Carnegie course while working at Die Supplies, Inc. "Taking this course helped me immensely in my career. Certainly, it helped me get better at speaking to groups of people, and people I did not know," he said. In later years, he became a vendor at Macsteel—the steel company was purchased years later and was renamed Gerdau Macsteel. "I was beyond startled when they selected Temple Supply to be their Fort Smith plant's only supplier for their maintenance crew's requirements," Mr. Word fondly remembers. "It instantly made the Industrial Supply Division of Temple successful, and the steel company became the main profit producer for Temple Supply. It eventually was the main reason that the Fort Smith Purchasing Managers awarded me their Salesman of the Year award."

Mr. Word soon reaped the fruits of his hard work and his ability to build relationships with those working in the industry blossomed. Word revealed, "The Purchasing Management Association (PMA) told Mr. Temple that I had won the award, but the management team kept it a secret from me. Mr. Temple invited me and the management team to attend the annual PMA banquet. The PMA had a former Senator and Presidential Candidate, Dale Bumpers, to be their keynote speaker. I was shocked when Dale Bumpers invited me to come onto the stage where he presented me with the 1984 PMA Salesman of the Year award.

The Clayton House

Bill Kincannon retired a few years after this, and I became the Industrial Supply Division Manager. We opened a Branch operation in Springdale. I know several people that I hired and helped train that are now very successful in varied industries. It always makes me happy to hear their success stories. More than one says that they still use the motto that I preached to them—Plan your work and work your Plan." Mr. Word worked for Temple Supply for seventeen years until they sold the company to Arkansas Mill Supply headquartered in Pine Bluff, Arkansas.

Mr. Word volunteered on every other Saturday prior to his retirement. "I knew that I wanted to stay busy after retirement, and I wanted to be sure that I enjoyed what I was doing. I did enjoy telling visitors from all over the world about Miss Laura's house and the places to enjoy in Fort Smith," said Word.

"After I retired, I stopped volunteering at Miss Laura's and devoted my time volunteering at the Fort Smith Museum of History, mainly telling school groups historical facts about Fort Smith. I also volunteer at the Clayton House, portraying W.H.H. Clayton on special occasions. Before Clayton became a judge, he was Judge Parker's prosecuting attorney. I am also active with the True Grit Trail organization. I serve as their host in

Fort Smith Museum of History

Fort Smith. I am currently serving my second term as president of the Fort Smith Historical Society."

Mr. Bill Word is still cultivating his innate gift for making connections with others to make a positive impact in Fort Smith, Arkansas!

Works Cited

"Fort Smith Museum of History." *Arkansas Department of Parks, Heritage, and Tourism,* www.arkansas.com/fort-smith/museums-libraries/fort-smith museum-history. Accessed 20 Mar. 2025.

"Welcome to The Clayton House." *The Clayton House,* claytonhouse.org/. Accessed 21 Mar. 2025.

Mr. Tom Wing, M.Ed. – Director & Assistant Professor, History Social Sciences of Philosophy, University of Arkansas - Fort Smith

Lord Byron said, in his satirical poem titled *Don Juan* that "Truth is stranger than fiction." Truth can also be enlightening, interesting, inspiring, and much more!

Mr. Tom Wing, director of the Drennen-Scott Historic Site and assistant professor of History at the University of Arkansas - Fort Smith (UAFS) has a passion for researching and uncovering historical facts in our region.

Mr. Wing was born in 1964 in Fort Smith, Arkansas, to Joe and Shirley Wing. His father was a firefighter. Inspired by his father's service to others, Mr. Wing became a Park Ranger. He is a product of Fort Smith Schools, where he attended Kimmons Junior High School and Westark Community College.

Wing has been married to his wife, Renee, for thirty-six years, and they have four sons and seven grandchildren. He earned two bachelor's degrees from the University of Arkansas, a master's from the University of Oklahoma, and he

By Sage Hardie - eleventh-grade scholar at Northside High School

has been working on a PhD at Stephen F. Austin State University in Texas

His inspiration comes from his father. "He taught me to study what I love," shared Wing. "My father pushed me to do what I love. Everyone can be fixed on something. Don't take "No" for an answer and apply yourself." Taking his father's advice, Mr. Wing has dedicated himself to conducting research, writing articles and books, and making people knowledgeable about the unique history of our communities. For instance, Mr. Wing has conducted extensive research on the Drennen family of Van Buren, Arkansas. The Drennen home and its historic contents were purchased by UAFS and the Arkansas Department of Heritage in 2005. "I proposed the Drennen-Scott project and got approval to move forward from the University of Arkansas - Fort Smith. Taking on the role as grant-writer and writing a series of four grants totaling five point three million dollars, I was moved to Project Director from 2005–2010, and then Site Director from 2011 to present," Wing detailed.

John Drennen is a unique character in the history of Van Buren and Arkansas. "There are several interesting, ironic facts about John Drennen's life. On one hand, he would be considered a Northerner (from Pennsylvania) in the years leading up to the Civil War, yet he lived most of his life in the South and considered himself a Southerner. He was a Whig in his political views, which made him a

Drennen-Scott House Van Buren, Arkansas

liberal in his day rather than a conservative. Whigs were in the minority in the South," Wing explained. "He was in simple terms a slave-owning, Northern, Liberal, Whig. This made him even more ironic and atypical in his day. He possessed excellent business skills and was successful in a variety of profitable ventures." According to Wing, John Drennen's prestige was evident in multiple sectors. Drennen's influence was not just shown locally, his prestige had a long reach. "His friends included two Presidents, James K. Polk and Zachary Taylor. He was a friend and partner with Sam Houston of Texas fame, and his lawyer and close friend was Albert Pike," said Wing. Drennen's slave owning history, and his work for the government as an agent to the Cherokee and Choctaw tribes give us important details of the time.

When asked why history preservation is so important, Mr. Wing replied, "It is important to preserve history because in understanding the past, we can see the effects and consequences of decisions that affect us today. We can see causes and long-term effects, and solutions, some successful and some not. History tells us where we have been and where we are going. Historic sites and buildings are a tangible link to our collective past and help define us as a people, good and bad things included."

Major Achievements

- Becoming a Park Ranger and Historian

- Full-time professor at UAFS in 2004

- Gaining approval for the Drennen-Scott Project

- Approval of a five-point-three-million-dollar grant for the Drennen Project

- Drennen - Scott Project Director 2005–2010

- Drennen-Scott Site Director 2011–present

- Co-author of the historical fiction book, *Julia and Maud* (2023)

Works Cited

Joenks, Laurinda. "Van Buren Treasure Drennen-Scott House Preserves History of Five Generations." *Arkansas Democrat-Gazette*, 10 Mar. 2016, www.arkansasonline.com/news/2016/mar/10/van-buren-treasure-20160310/. Accessed 19 Mar. 2025.

"UAFS Drennen-Scott Historic Site 150 Years of History in a Working Laboratory." *Visit Van Buren Arkansas*, www.vanburen.org/uafs-drennen-scott-house/. Accessed 19 Mar. 2025.

Jody and Rachael Presson, Coaches – Greenwood High School

"Champions aren't made in gyms. Champions are made from something they have deep inside of them—a desire, a dream, a vision" attributed to Muhammad Ali.

Rachael Presson was born in September 1979, and her husband, Jody Presson, was born in September 1981, both in Fort Smith, Arkansas. Rachael was raised in Greenwood, Arkansas. Jody was raised in Waldron, Arkansas. The Pressons were married in July 2001. They have one daughter, Taryn Presson. Taryn was valedictorian of the Greenwood class of 2024. She is a nineteen-year-old freshman at Brown University. She is majoring in political science, and she wants to become a lawyer.

Jody Presson attended Westark Community College, which became the University of Arkansas - Fort Smith (UAFS) He was not the best student because he says he was lazy and he just didn't want to apply himself academically, but that changed when he met his future wife, Rachael. Rachael was working on earning an associate degree at Westark Community College, while cheering there for four years. Later, she earned a bachelor's degree in business administration at Arkansas State University. Rachael

By Aiden Pope - tenth-grade scholar at Northside High School

has a teacher's license in math and physical education. Once married, Jody commuted between Greenwood and Russellville, where he earned a bachelor's degree from Arkansas Tech University. He has a teacher's license in history and physical education.

This is the twentieth year of Jody Presson's career. He taught one year at the Arkansas Department of Corrections, eleven years at Darby Junior High School, and eight years at Greenwood Schools. Rachael worked for six years at Clear Channel Outdoor, taught math for six years at Greenwood, coached cheer at Darby Junior High School for five years, and coached cheer for the past eight years at Greenwood Schools.

For fun and adventure, the Pressons spend time traveling. They have visited all fifty states and eleven countries. Rachael likes to spend time reading and collecting vintage Barbies, and Jody likes to collect sports memorabilia.

The Pressons are the perfect match in the elite world of cheer! Both motivate students in the classroom and in the sport of cheer. "We built the Darby cheer program from the ground up, taking eighth and ninth grade girls with little to no experience to the best in the state," stated Coach Jody Presson. "We have coached cheer for thirteen years. Our first five years were at Darby Junior High in Fort Smith, and the next eight have been at Greenwood Junior and Senior High Schools. We also restarted the dance team at Darby after a twelve-year hiatus. We just finished winning our second straight state championship at Greenwood High School after many years of success on the junior high level. We have always built our programs based on dedication, commitment, hard work, and love. We believe in a family environment and helping the kids develop into something they can be proud of."

The Pressons credit their mentors for nurturing, modeling, and instilling the ideas that have influenced them as coaches, teachers, and role models. Rick May coached Jody. "I looked up to him, and I wanted to be like him one day," said Coach Jody. Coach Rachael's high school cheer coach, Martina Peacock, set the example that she follows today. "She was strict, and she set high expectations," said Coach Rachael. The Pressons have taken the lessons they have learned and have become the coaches of champions!

Coach Rachael missed cheering, so she wanted to jump back into the community. Coach Rachael always had the dream to become a coach and to be involved in some type of a sport. "I like to see people achieve their goals by teaching them a good work ethic," said Coach Rachael. "I hope it will help them later in life to become well-rounded adults."

Coach Rachael said, "I enjoy teaching teamwork to help young people achieve their goals, and helping kids become the best they can be."

The Greenwood High School Bulldog Cheer squad won state titles in 2023 and 2024. All their hard work and perseverance took the cheer squad to the next level. The team won the 2025 NCA title at nationals in Dallas, Texas, a first for the school. This achievement came only five weeks after winning their second state title. The Pressons' dream of winning a national championship in cheer finally came true!

2025 NCA National Champions!
Greenwood High School Cheer Team
Jan. 2025 in Dallas, TX.

Emily Arthur, Laura Bankuti, Harper Berg, Jaylen Bollinger, Luke Brandt, Lainey Brewer, Jace Brown, Clara Burton, Emmy Burton, Zoe Caldwell, Elizabeth Caraway, Emery Driscoll, Meri Grace Finley, Tori Hastings, Rylin Hendrickson, AddiBelle Holloway, Emma Grace McCubbin, Emma Ramsey, Kate Salmon, Katelyn Sanchez, Mackenzie Skaggs, Kailyn Tarrant, Ella Thompson, Kenadee Thompson, Kenze Vines, Blayne West, Brooklin West and Coaches Jody & Rachael Presson

Managers: Lyla Brewer / Mascot: Afrodita Bohorquez

Major Achievements

- 2015 Junior High Northeast Arkansas Cheer Classic Champions, 6A-7A Division - Darby Junior High Cheerleaders - sponsored by B2 Cheer in Paragould, AR on Nov. 14. Also, awarded first place for Top Pyramid, and for The Tough Man competition out of all junior and senior high schools in the competition.

- 2015 Junior High ACCA Cheer Classic Champions, 7A Division - Darby Junior High Cheerleaders - at Mayflower High School on December 12. Also awarded first place for Best Dance and Best Stunts.

- 2015 Junior High Best of the Best State Champions, 7A Division - Darby Junior High School Cheerleaders - at the Bank of the Ozarks Arena on Dec. 16 in Hot Springs, AR.

- 2016 Junior High Northeast Arkansas Cheer Class Champions, 6A-7A Division-Darby Junior High Cheerleaders - in Paragould, AR on November 12. Accolades include Best Choreography, Best Stunts, Best Jumps, and Best Cheer.

- 2016 Junior High ACCA Cheer Classic Champions, 7A Division -Darby Junior High Cheerleaders - in Mayflower, AR on December 10.

- 2016 Junior High Best of the Best State Champions, 7A Division - Darby Junior High School Cheerleaders - at the Bank of the Ozarks Arena in Hot Springs, AR on December 13. Other accolades included: Best Cheer, Best Choreography, Best Jumps, and Grand Champions.

- 2017 Championship Ring Ceremony at Darby Junior High School on April 13, 2016. School officials, family, and friends celebrated the numerous accomplishments of the cheerleaders, the Pressons, and the team managers for performing at the elite level during the 2015 and 2016 seasons of cheer.

- April 13, 2017, declared Darby Junior High School Cheerleaders' Day in the City of Fort Smith by former Mayor Sandy Sanders.

- 2023 State Champions – Greenwood High School Cheerleaders - Bank OZK Arena in Hot Springs on December 15, 2023.

- 2024 State Champions – Greenwood High School Cheerleaders - Bank OZK Arena in Hot Springs on December 20, 2024.

- 2025 National Champions - Greenwood High School Cheerleaders - Kay Bailey Hutchison Convention Center in Dallas, TX, on January 25-26, 2025.

Memory Lane

2015 State Champions
Darby Junior High School Cheer Squad
Northeast Arkansas Cheer Classic Competition

AnnMarie Diaz, Elisabeth Abeyta, Diana Ramirez, Lorena Sanabria, Aaliyah Huff, and Yanira Laguna, Dede Swinson, Sierra Wise, Maricela Garcia, Jocelyn Ayala, Mariela "Haha" Delpozo, Shameila Jones, Shykira Sampson, Abby Hope, Michelle Pedraza, Angelia Christian and Coaches Jody & Rachael Presson

State Champions 6A/7B Division
Darby Junior High Cheer Squad
2015 Northeast Arkansas Cheer Classic Competition
Sponsored by B2 Competition
Paragould, AR on Nov. 14, 2015

AnnMarie Diaz, Elisabeth Abeyta, Diana Ramirez, Lorena Sanabria, Aaliyah Huff, Yanlra Laguna, Dede Swinson, Sierra Wise, Maricela Garcia, Jocelyn Ayala, Mariela "Haha" Delpozo, Shameila Jones, Shykira Sampson, Abby Hope, Michelle Pedraza, Angelia Christian
and Coaches Jody & Rachael Presson

First place: "Tough Man Competition" by holding an extension for the longest duration of time: Dede Swinson, Diana Ramirez, Aaliyah Huff and Abby Hope.

First place: "Best Stunt" by Shameila Jones, Lorena Sanabria, AnnMarie Diaz and Angelia Christian.

Managers: Jayla Alston, Deysy Esquivel and Taryn Presson.

State Champions 7A Division
Darby Junior High School Cheer Squad
2016 AACA Cheer Classic
Mayflower, AR on Nov. 12, 2016

Jocelyn Ayala, Angelia Christian, Jomara Cordero, AnnMarie Diaz, Aaliyah Huff, Xandria Hutson, Molly Johnson, Shameila Jones, Caroline King, Isabella Pope, Makyra Robinson, Shykira Sampson and Dede Swinson.

Managers: Jayla Alston, Deysy Esquivel and Taryn Presson.

State Champions 7A Division
Darby Junior High School Cheer Squad
2016 AACA Cheer Classic
Paragould, AR on December 10, 2016

Best Cheer and Best Choreography

Third Place: "Tough Woman Competition"—Aaliyah Huff, Shameila Jones and Angelia Christian

State Champions
Darby Junior High Cheer Squad
2016 Arkansas Junior High Best of the Best Championship
Bank of the Ozarks Arena
Hot Springs, AR, on December 16, 2016

Jocelyn Ayala, Angelia Christian, Jomara Cordero, AnnMarie Diaz, Aaliyah Huff, Xandria Hutson, Molly Johnson, Shameila Jones, Caroline King, Isabella Pope, Makyra Robinson, Shykira Sampson and Dede Swinson.

Managers: Jayla Alston, Deysy Esquivel and Taryn Presson.

First Place: Best Cheer, Best Choreography and Best Jumps.

***Darby Junior Cheer Champion Ring Ceremony for Two Consecutive
State Championships
2015 - 2016***

Jocelyn Ayala, Angelia Christian, Jomara Cordero, AnnMarie Diaz, Aaliyah
Huff, Xandria Hutson, Molly Johnson, Shameila Jones, Caroline King,
Isabella Pope, Makyra Robinson, Shykira Sampson, Dede Swinson
and Coach Jody & Rachael Presson.

Managers: Jayla Alston, Deysy Esquivel and Taryn Presson.

The 2017 Darby Parent Cheer Committee hosted a fundraiser to raise twenty-five hundred dollars to purchase championship rings to bestow to the Pressons, the cheer squad, and the team managers in honor of two consecutive years of winning state championships. Attendees included: Principal Katie Kreimer-Hall, Dr. Brubaker, superintendent, Dr. Floyd Owen, members of the School Board, Rep. Justin Boyd (R), Rep. George B. McGill (D), the late Charlotte Tidwell, Antioch for Youth & Families and other leaders in business & religious organizations. Ms. Bobbie Woodard represented former Mayor Sandy Sanders office and declared April 13, 2017, *Darby Junior High School Cheerleaders' Day.*

Artwork by Contributors

Representing Mr. Jerry H. Moore

By Josianne Gentry - twelfth-grade scholar at Southside High School

Representing Ms. Sherry Lee (Brown) Toliver

By Tooba Sehr – twelfth-grade scholar at Southside High School

Representing Floyd and Sue Robison

By Lucas White - ninth-grade scholar at Southside High School

Representing Mrs. Denise Joan Johnson

By Tori Smith - eleventh-grade scholar at Southside High School

Representing Mr. Tracy Christian

By Elizabeth Tore - tenth-grade scholar at Southside High School

Representing Mr. Tom Shay

By Kassidy Badger - tenth-grade scholar at Northside High School

Representing Dr. Steve-Felix Belinga

By Josianne Gentry - twelfth-grade scholar at Southside High School

Representing Mrs. Katherine Brown

By Aiden Pope - tenth-grade scholar at Northside High School

Representing Mr. Billy D. Higgins

By Kylie Davis - tenth-grade scholar at Southside High School

Representing Dr. A. Naseer Adjei

By Aiden Pope - tenth-grade scholar at Northside High School

Representing Dr. Carolyn Mosley

By Kassidy Badger - tenth-grade scholar at Northside High School

Representing Mayor George McGill

By Kassidy Badger - tenth-grade scholar at Northside High School

Representing Chief Danny Baker

By Jason Peraza - tenth-grade scholar at Northside High School

Representing Mrs. Dorothy Johnson

By Josh Chung - eleventh-grade scholar at Southside High School

Representing Mrs. Judy Christian

By Sage Hardie - eleventh-grade scholar at Northside High School

Representing Mrs. Trish Richardson

By Jason Peraza - tenth-grade scholar at Northside High School

Representing Mrs. Angela Walton-Raji

By Josh Chung - eleventh-grade scholar at Southside High School

Representing Mrs. Cosaundra Chapple

By Aiden Pope - tenth-grade scholar at Northside High School

Representing Ms. Cathy Triplett

By Tammy Nguyen -twelfth-grade scholar at Southside High School

Representing Mr. Bill Word

By Tarissa Thibodeaux – eleventh-grade scholar at Northside High School

Representing Mr. Tom Wing

By Sage Hardie - eleventh-grade scholar at Northside High School

Representing Coaches Jody and Rachael Presson

By Aiden Pope - tenth-grade scholar at Northside High School

Celebrate! Maya Project Launch and Workshops

The History Makers launch was held at the University of Arkansas - Fort Smith on January 25, 2025. The event introduced the many sponsors of the Maya Project.

Mrs. Judy Christian– Project launch emcee

Maya Project Sponsors

*Mrs. Joyce Faulkner
(Red Engine Press)*

*Mr. David King – Art Teacher at
Southside High School*

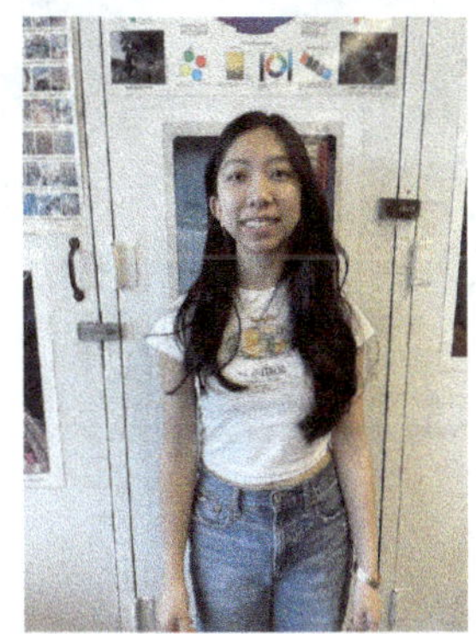

Tammy Nguyen – Cover Artist

The Maya Project writers' workshop was held at the Wesley United Methodist Church on February 8,2025. The artists' workshop was held at the Fort Smith Regional Art Museum on March 15, 2025. These workshops were help sessions for the scholars as they prepared for their interview and artwork of the history makers. The following images are of the activities during the events.

Ms. Shelly Blanton, Archivest, The Pebley Center, UAFS
Keynote Speaker at the Writing Workshop

Daisy Raya is a tenth-grade scholar at Northside High School. She is also a member of the Northside High School Photography Club that is sponsored by Ms. Leigh Ann Hasley. The Celebrate! Maya Project would like to thank Daisy for her contributions during the launch on January 25, 2025, at the University of Arkansas - Fort Smith.

Homes of History
by Mr. Tom Wing

Drennen-Scott Home

In 1836, John Drennen and his brother-in-law, David Thompson, bought almost six hundred acres on the north bank of the Arkansas River in Crawford County. A small village named Phillips Landing was included in the deal. In 2005, the University of Arkansas - Fort Smith (UAFS), through grant funding, purchased the remaining thirty-six acres of the original tract, plus John Drennen's house, built in 1838, and handed down through his family for five generations. While a home with that sort of history, triumphs and tragedies, victories and failures, lean times, and hard times, is compelling, John Drennen is much more.

Born to an Irish immigrant who fought in the American Revolution, John Drennen left home in Elizabeth, Pennsylvania when he became "of age." He first found opportunity and a new wife and family in Nashville, Tennessee. He married a widow, Emily Dederick Stuart, and they eventually had three children. In Nashville, he partnered with his brother-in-law, David Thompson, and operated a mercantile store near the state capitol. While in Nashville, Drennen fostered business and personal relationships with historical figures like Sam Houston and James K. Polk. Looking for more lucrative opportunities, Drennen and Thompson moved their store to Little Rock in the mid 1820s but pushed further west to Crawford County.

Thompson and Drennen are considered the founders of Van Buren. After acquiring the land in 1836, Thompson died the next year and did not see the development of the town. Before his death, the two platted the future streets and advertised in the Arkansas Gazette newspaper to attract developers and people to populate the new town. With no bridge across the river, Drennen quickly secured the ferry business, which moved agricultural products, the U.S. Mail, and the Butterfield Stage to Fort Smith and beyond. In those days, Crawford County was one of the largest in the state and included parts of Washington and Sebastian Counties as well as land that is today Oklahoma.

Drennen represented Crawford County at the statehood convention in 1836 and served in the first state legislature in 1837. His efforts to have Van Buren named County Seat were rewarded after he donated a square block in the town for the courthouse, constructed in 1842. He continued to promote civic development in Van Buren by donating ten acres for Fairview Cemetery. His business ventures brought many steamboats to Crawford County and helped connect the area to the population centers back east. Goods, products, information and news all came by steamboat to be dispersed through the new town of Van Buren. Drennen also saw the future benefit of railroads and became a founding stockholder of the Little Rock & Fort Smith Railroad—tracks that are still used today.

While Drennen's fingerprints are on much of the county, and still visible, his story is not always positive. Drennen owned land in twenty-seven counties in Arkansas; foreclosures he bought for cents on the acre after recovery by the Real Estate Bank, of which he was a board member. He was brought into court numerous times on behalf of the shady bank practices and his own land transactions. He operated a cotton plantation in Chicot County that included one thousand acres of some of the best farmland in Arkansas and held around one hundred slaves to work his fields. He also had ten to fifteen domestic servants, held in bondage at his home in Van Buren. One of the slaves kept in Van Buren served as a body servant, (butler, carriage driver, bodyguard). Through research it was discovered that Patrick Drennen is buried in the Drennen-Scott family plot at Fairview Cemetery. Patrick has living descendants who regularly contribute to the historical interpretation of the site.

The input of slave descendants enriches our understanding of the complexities of the past and helps us to consider all the important perspectives of the Drennen-Scott story. Also, on the negative side, Drennen was selected to serve as Indian Agent to the Choctaw Nation in 1849. In 1851, he was promoted to Superintendent of Indian Affairs for the region and had authority over the Five Tribes and others. This appointment made Drennen an instrument of Federal Indian policy, as he dealt with some of the consequences of the "Trail of Tears," a time of tragedy and loss for Native Americans. Drennen-Scott documents the second-class nature of women for much of its history, and the difficulties faced by women to fit into a world where men had greater status. Through this, we can consider the positive and negative aspects of our collective past and hopefully find ways to heal and learn from the events and people.

After acquiring the property in 2005, UAFS has meticulously preserved and restored the property, transforming the home into a museum and educational facility. Students of all ages, have studied, researched, served as interns, published articles, and participated in educational programs aimed at honoring and understanding the complexities of the past. As a public museum, Drennen-Scott adds to the local and regional heritage tourism economy, engaging the public in all aspects of the story. The site has won awards for historic preservation and has been recognized by the Governor for contributions to tourism. The staff has received awards for historic preservation education, and for promoting and preserving the history of Arkansas.

Drennen-Scott Historic Site is open April–November, hosts a monthly lecture series, and can be rented for special tours, meetings, and events.

Willhaf Home

Starting in 2015, through the private donation of Sandra Pearson and Melissa Wick, and funding from the Arkansas Natural and Cultural Resources Council, the University of Arkansas - Fort Smith (UAFS) has worked through the Covid Pandemic and a total of five phases ($2.6 million) to restore the 1851 home of Leonard Willhaf.

Leonard was a German immigrant to Arkansas, bakery owner in Van Buren, and veteran of the Mexican War. During the Mexican War he was the flag bearer of the Crawford County Company of Archibald Yell's Mounted Rifles. He was promoted to Lieutenant before the end of the conflict. The flag Willhaf carried was presented to the soldiers on the lawn of the Crawford County Courthouse in Van Buren by the ladies' association who sewed it and is currently part of the collection of the Old State House. UAFS Assistant Professor of History, Tom Wing and John Milner and Associates, Director of Preservation, John Mott conducted extensive historical research, engaged the Arkansas Archeological Survey, the Dendrochronology Laboratory at the University of Arkansas, and a host of other preservation professionals to document, preserve original material, and restore the property to the original 1850s appearance. One of the interesting findings was a newspaper article that documented the planting of a Magnolia tree in 1851 that still stands next to the house. The home is open for tours to provide a sharp historical contrast, from an interpretive standpoint, telling the story of a working class, immigrant family in Arkansas, as opposed to the elite and well to do, Drennen-Scott family just across the tracks and up the hill. The Willhaf property helps complete the 19th century interpretation of Van Buren and western Arkansas.

The Willhaf house is promoted by the Van Buren Advertising and Promotions Commission, and the project was aided by a partnership with the City of Van Buren for water and sewer upgrades, as well as pedestrian sidewalks for visitor access. The Willhaf property is also available for rental use as small group meetings, receptions and events.

Leonard and his wife (formerly Mary Beckel) were part of an early nineteenth century wave of German immigrants to the United States. It is believed Leonard came through St. Louis, Missouri then down into Arkansas while Mary had ties to Fort Smith from the beginning, through extended family including the Reutzel clan.

Leonard died in 1866 and is buried in Fairview Cemetery in Van Buren. Mary expanded the home to include rooms to board transient railroad workers. Archeology work onsite revealed the locations of foundations of this long-lost addition. After Mary's passing, the home was sold and eventually occupied by Ora Smith. Ora was a history teacher in the Fort Smith Public School district and a local historian of note. Ora lived in the Willhaf House for many years and secured a National Register Nomination for the home. Ora died without heirs and the final owners of the house were John and Zoe Cobb. Sandra Pearson and Melissa Wick inherited the property after the passing of their father and donated the home to UAFS for preservation and restoration.

The partnership with the City of Van Buren and the Van Buren Advertising and Promotions Commission are proof that the Willhaf and Drennen-Scott properties are an important part of the heritage tourism product for Van Buren and Western Arkansas., The historical restoration project put millions of dollars back into the local economy as a Van Buren firm (Crawford Construction) was the general contractor and many local subcontractors were used for the project.

The site includes a nineteenth century vegetable garden which will be maintained through a partnership of Van Buren Public Schools, Master Gardeners, and UAFS.

The Willhaf House as it appeared in 1857

Sandra Pearson (L), and Melissa Wick (R), Van Buren Mayor Joe Hurst in the background.

The Magnolia tree planted in 1851

Evening at the Willhaf House

(all photographs provided by Mr. Tom Wing)

Epilogue

David King, Art Teacher, Southside High School

I was born in Fort Smith, raised here, and now teach art at one of our city's two public high schools. I believe it is important to hear the stories of people who have made a significant impact on the River Valley and surrounding areas. This book tells the stories of some of those people. It was very inspiring to hear these History Makers speak about their experiences when we began this process. Their passion for their specific causes and drive to serve the community was powerful. It was my hope that the students who participated would be able to capture that passion and drive in their individual artworks. It was rewarding to see these students, some with no past art experience, push themselves to create honorable tributes to these History Makers from our region.

Angela Stout, English Teacher, Instructional Chair, Southside High School

As an English teacher at Southside, I often use historical texts (fiction and nonfiction) as core reading material for analysis. This practice is important because it is vital that our students know and understand history from all regions and ethnic groups. What excites me about this project is that the participating students interviewed primary sources of Fort Smith and River Valley history and wrote essays documenting them. The experiences shared by the interviewees are now published for posterity. For decades to come, people can learn about the history of our area from those who not only lived it but also made an impact while doing so. Our students and anyone who reads this book will discover how to work hard, persevere, and care about others in their community.

Nichelle Christian, English Teacher, Northside High School

I have been teaching grade eleven English at NHS since 2021. It has been a rewarding experience to see these scholars, from rival high schools, take on the role of interviewers to document the rich histories of those who have positively impacted Fort Smith, Arkansas, and the surrounding regions! I am grateful to Ms. Janis F. Kearney and the Celebrate! Maya Project for featuring the River Valley in her statewide initiative to preserve the past while giving scholars a meaningful real-life experience to add depth to their academic skills. Our group of volunteers who stepped up to serve on a collaborative planning committee made all the difference in making this project a success!

I hope these scholars cultivate a lasting interest in honoring the past with a hope of preserving history, whether it be in their families or communities, for years to come!

Floyd and Sue Robison

We were raised on opposite sides of Fort Smith when that was like living in different worlds. Years after growing up, moving away, coming home and meeting as adults, a mutual love for Fort Smith helped bring us together. Fort Smith has a fascinating past, and it is our honor as a couple to share it with youngsters and adults. We see how much Fort Smith honors its history but, more importantly, we see the city's bright and promising future being created by students like those involved in the Celebrate! Maya project.

What a grand conglomeration of people we are, and what a wonderful way to celebrate our differences. Celebrate! Maya project is an accounting of our past. These students are a promise to the future.

Ms. Sherry Toliver

It was exciting to be on the planning committee for the Celebrate! Maya Project. The documentation and preservation of our history have been my passion for the last thirty years. I was asked to identify Fort Smith History Makers. Since I was president of the Fort Smith Historical Society for many years, this was an easy job.

Everyone I contacted was happy to participate. Seniors loved to tell their stories to the younger generation and the students were eager to learn from them. What a brilliant idea to have students interview senior citizens! The "History Makers" stories and pictures will be published in a book and available for all to enjoy—thanks to John & Joyce Faulkner, Red Engine Press Publishing Company.

The Celebrate! Maya Project is a "Win/Win" for all involved.

Special Thanks to Ms. Janice Kearney and Mrs. Nichelle Christian for choosing Fort Smith for this honor. Thank you to the History Makers, students, teachers, supporters and volunteers. You all have been simply amazing!

Mr. Billy D. Higgins

If as Francis Bacon said long ago, "Knowledge is Power" then the Maya Angelou Initiative served student-scholars and senior citizens well by getting them together in a meaningful way to record memories. It has been said as well that knowledge comes from seeking and brings happiness. So nice going to all who participated as interviewers, history-makers, sponsors, directors, and publishers. You have added significantly to Arkansas' history.

Mr. Bill Word

I served on the planning committee for the River Valley Celebrate! Maya Project. I was able to see what a great statewide program that Janis F. Kearney brought to our area. It was impressive to see the professionalism and organization that she presented to our group. I saw how dedicated the instructors are, and how talented the students are with their written work, and how creative they are with their artwork. It was amazing how quickly volunteers from all corners of our city worked together and did what was needed to make our meetings comfortable, and meals provided in abundance. The sponsors and supporters quickly and graciously provided the facilities and any support that was needed. Seeing this from the start certainly makes me feel "Fort Smith Proud and River Valley Strong", to quote our great Mayor and History Maker, George McGill. What a wonderful community we live in! As President of the Fort Smith Historical Society, I hope that we can continue identifying the History Makers in our community and recording their story.

Acknowledgements
Sponsors and Supporters

The Belinga Foundation

Celebrate! Maya Project

Fort Smith Historical Society

Fort Smith Museum of History

Fort Smith Public Schools

Fort Smith Regional Art Museum

The Housewives of Fort Smith

Lincoln Youth Service Center

Mission United Methodist Church

Northside High School (NHS)

NHS Photography Club

Phillis Wheatley Club

Red Engine Press

Southside High School (SHS)

True Grit Trail

Unity Missionary Baptist Church
University of Arkansas - Fort Smith

Wesley United Methodist Church

Celebrate! Maya Project Planning Committee

Mrs. Nichelle Christian	English Teacher, NHS, and Community and School Coordinator
Dr. Brittany Hudson	Community Facilitator
Ms. Dorothy Johnson	Community Facilitator
Ms. Janis F. Kearney	Founder and President
Mr. David King	Art Teacher, SHS, and Art and School Coordinator
Rep. Jay Richardson	Community Facilitator
Mrs. Talicia Richardson	Community Facilitator
Mrs. Sue Robison	Community Facilitator
Mr. Floyd Robison	Community Facilitator
Ms. Caroline Speir	Executive Director, Fort Smith Museum of History
Ms. Angela Stout	Dept. Chair, English, SHS, and School Coordinator
Ms. Sherry Lee (Brown) Toliver	Community Facilitator
Mr. Bill Word	Community Facilitator

Fort Smith Regional Art Museum Event